AMERICAN SOCIETY FOR TRAINING & DEVELOPMENT

WILLIAM J. ROTHWELL
ETHAN S. SANDERS
JEFFREY G. SOPER

ASTD MODELS FOR WORKPLACE LEARNING AND PERFORMANCE

ROLES, COMPETENCIES, AND OUTPUTS

D1313954

ASTD

Ordering Information: Books published by the American Society for Training & Development can be ordered by calling 800.628.2783.

1640 King Street
Box 1443
Alexandria, VA 22313-2043
PH 703.683.8100, FX 703.683.8103
www.astd.org

Library of Congress Catalog Card Number: 98-74603

ISBN: 1-56286-110-7

TABLE OF CONTENTS

LIST OF TABLES AND FIGURES

◢ ACKNOWLEDGMENTS

Expert Panel on Workplace Learning and Performance[1]

ASTD Models for Workplace Learning and Performance is based on a study conducted in 1997–1998 by William J. Rothwell, Ethan S. Sanders, and Jeffrey G. Soper. We would like to thank the many dedicated individuals who participated in our data collection effort, without whose help and support this study would not have been possible. In particular, we would like to thank the members of the line manager and workplace learning and performance (WLP) expert groups, who completed the questionnaire and supplied us with invaluable insight into the future of this profession. Those individuals are listed below in alphabetical order by group.

WLP Expert Respondent Group

Robert Barthelemy
Director
Taos Laboratories
Dayton, OH

Henry Berman
Consultant
First Light Media Group
Needham, MA

Melinda Bickerstaff
Director, Financial Services Consulting
KPMG
Bethesda, MD

Elaine Biech
Partner
EBB Associates
Portage, WI

Mary Broad
Principal Consultant
Performance Excellence
Chevy Chase, MD

W. Warner Burke
Chairman
W. Warner Burke Associates, Inc.
Pelham, NY

Susan Burnett
Manager, Executive Education & Development
Hewlett Packard Company
Palo Alto, CA

Paul H. Chaddock
Management Consultant
Ipswich, MA

Neal Chalofsky
Associate Professor, HRD
The George Washington University
Washington, DC

Richard Chang
Chief Executive Officer
Richard Chang Associates, Inc.
Irvine, CA

Stephen Cohen
President and CEO
The Learning Design Group
Minneapolis, MN

Gary Craig
Senior Consultant
Vector Group, Inc.
Longmont, CO

Barbara Nobles Crawford
Nobles Crawford & Partners
Framingham, MA

Jan Danford
Manager, New Product Launch Training
General Motors
Lansing, MI

James DeVito
Vice President, Educational Research and Services
Johnson & Johnson
New Brunswick, NJ

Ronald Galbraith
President
Management 21, Inc.
Nashville, TN

Gene Hahne
Chief Executive Officer
Intercom
Houston, TX

---

[1] *The participation of the following individuals does not constitute their agreement or disagreement with the results of this study.*

Michael Hansen
Director
The MITRE Corporation
McLean, VA

Kenneth Hanson
Vice President and Assistant Director
Motorola Inc.
Schaumburg, IL

Marlys Hanson
Principal
Hanson and Associates
Livermore, CA

Richard Headley
Vice President and Dean
Fisher University
Fisher Scientific Company
Pittsburgh, PA

Linda Hodo
HRD Consultant Unit Manager
Hewitt Associates
Lincolnshire, IL

Peggy Hutcheson
President
The Odyssey Group
Atlanta, GA

David Jamieson
President
Jamieson Consulting Group
Los Angeles, CA

Joanne Jorz
Vice President—Program Development
Conceptual Systems, Inc.
Silver Spring, MD

W. Mathew Juechter
Chief Executive Officer
ARC International
Denver, CO

Gary Jusela
Corporate Director
The Boeing Company
Seattle, WA

Donald Kirkpatrick
Professor Emeritus
University of Wisconsin
Elm Grove, WI

Karin Kolodzieiski
Partner
MetaSkills Consulting Group
Portland, OR

Nancy Kuhn
Vice President—Education and Training
American Red Cross
Arlington, VA

Ursula Lohmann
Dean of Academics
Army Management Staff College
Ft. Belvoir, VA

Jan Margolis
Managing Director
Applied Research Corporation
Metuchen, NJ

Michael Marquardt
Professor
The George Washington University
Washington, DC

Lynda McDermott
President
EquiPro International Ltd
New York, NY

Donna McNamara
Director, Global Education and Training
Colgate-Palmolive Company
New York, NY

Stephen Merman
Vice President
Right Management Consultants
Denver, CO

Robert Mjos
Manager—Development & Learning
Digital Equipment Corporation
Maynard, MA

John Newstrom
Professor of Management
University of Minnesota—Duluth
Duluth, MN

J. Edwin O'Brien
Director, Human Resource-CAV
Corning, Inc.
Corning, NY

Sylvia Odenwald
President
The Odenwald Connection Inc.
Garland, TX

Julie O'Mara
President
O'Mara and Associates
Castro Valley, CA

John Purnell
Managing Partner
Purnell Associates International
Cincinnati, OH

Gloria Regalbuto
Director of HR Development
Bath and Body Works
Columbus, OH

Carlene Reinhart
President
CLR Associates Inc.
Vienna, VA

Stephen Rhinesmith
President
Rhinesmith & Associates, Inc.
Boston, MA

Geary Rummler
Vice Chairman
Rummler Brache Group
Warren, NJ

Sally Sparhawk
President
Sparhawk Consulting
Rochester, NY

Line Managers

Mark Arnsberger
Booz, Allen & Hamilton
McLean, VA

Michael L. Baldwin
Johns Hopkins Hospital
Baltimore, MD

Robert M. Berzok
Union Carbide CT
Danbury, CT

Stephen Brown
The Black and Decker Corporation
Towson, MD

Paul Crawford
Booz, Allen & Hamilton
McLean, VA

Patricia Crull
McDonald's Corporation
Oak Brook, IL

Joyce C. Doria
Booz, Allen & Hamilton
McLean, VA

Audrey Drossner
Legg Mason
Baltimore, MD

Ann Durham
Provident Bank
Baltimore, MD

J. Robert Fluor II
Fluor Corporation
Irvine, CA

Anne M. Grier
Dominion Resources, Inc.
Richmond, VA

Ellen Grossman
Provident Bank
Baltimore, MD

Bill Henderson
Provident Bank
Baltimore, MD

Sue Horton
Booz, Allen & Hamilton
McLean, VA

Cindy Johnson
3M Corporation (Minnesota Mining and
    Manufacturing Company)
St, Paul, MN

T. Dennis Jorgensen
Tenet Healthcare Corporation
Santa Barbara, CA

Martin Kamber
ITT Industries, Inc.
White Plains, NY

Peter M. McGrath
JC Penney Company, Inc.
Plano, TX

John M. McLaughlen
CMS Generation Company
Dearborn, MI

William B. Oakley
Booz, Allen & Hamilton
McLean, VA

Jackie Oldham
Cadmus Journal Services
Linthicum, MD

Lucille Oricehio
PepsiCo, Inc.
Purchase, NY

Robert Post
Booz, Allen & Hamilton
McLean, VA

Zara Pyatt
Booz, Allen & Hamilton
McLean, VA

Susan S. Rickett
F&M Bank
New York, NY

Anil Savkar
Booz, Allen & Hamilton
McLean, VA

Susan Steele
McDonald's Corporation
Oak Brook, IL

Frank J. Steiner
Continental Airlines
Houston, TX

Karen Von Der Bruegge
Harrahs Entertainment, Inc.
Memphis, TN

Clifford O. Webster, Jr.
Provident Bank
Baltimore, MD

James Wallis
Provident Bank
Baltimore, MD

The members of the ASTD internal advisory review
panel are

- Philip Anderson
- Cynthia Hickman
- Greta Kotler
- Nancy Olson
- Ed Schroer
- Ruth Stadius
- Mark Van Buren.

The individuals from Pennsylvania State University
who provided research assistance are

- Chris Howard
- Daryl Hunt
- Hyug il Kwon
- Li Ning
- Hsiu-Ping Yueh.

ABOUT THE AUTHORS

William J. Rothwell

William J. Rothwell is professor of human resource development (HRD) in the Department of Adult Education, Instructional Systems and Workforce Education and Development, in the College of Education on the University Park Campus of The Pennsylvania State University. In that capacity he directs a graduate program in HRD. He is also director of Penn State's Institute for Research in Training and Development.

Rothwell is author, coauthor, editor, or coeditor of several publications including *Strategic Human Resource Leader* (1998, with Robert Prescott and Maria Taylor), *Mastering the Instructional Design Process* (2d ed., 1998, with H. C. Kazanas), *Beyond Instruction: Comprehensive Program Planning for Business and Education* (1997, with Peter S. Cookson), and *ASTD Models for Human Performance Improvement* (1996). He holds a Ph.D. from the University of Illinois at Urbana-Champaign and is accredited for life as a senior professional in human resources (SPHR). Rothwell has been a consultant for more than 30 *Fortune* 500 companies, including Motorola and Ford Motor Company (world headquarters). He can be reached at 647 Berkshire Drive, State College, PA 16803; phone: 814.234.6888; fax: 814.235.0528.

Ethan S. Sanders

Ethan S. Sanders is a senior project manager for The American Society for Training & Development (ASTD) in the Education Department. Before joining ASTD, he was a senior instructional designer of management development courses in the banking industry and a training manager in the transportation industry.

He is the coauthor of *ASTD Models for Learning Technologies* and the ASTD course Human Performance Improvement in the Workplace. Ethan also teaches several of ASTD's courses that are offered through corporate seminars. He holds a master's degree in applied behavioral science from the Johns Hopkins University. He can be reached at ASTD, 1640 King Street, Box 1443, Alexandria, VA 22313-2043; phone: 703.683.9595; e-mail: esanders@astd.org.

Jeffery G. Soper

Jeffrey G. Soper is an assistant professor of engineering leadership and the director of the engineering leadership development minor (ELDM) in the College of Engineering at the University Park campus of The Pennsylvania State University. He earned an M.B.A. from Columbia University and a doctorate degree in workforce education from The Pennsylvania State University.

From a practical perspective based on 23 years of industry and military experience, Soper speaks, consults, and conducts workshops and research in the areas of leadership, creativity, innovation, and change. He is the coauthor, with Jack Matson, of *Making Things C.L.I.C.K.*, an upcoming book on innovative leadership. Additionally, he codesigned, with John Hayden, the Web-based workplace learning and performance questionnaires and CD-ROM products for *ASTD Models for Learning Technologies* and this volume. He can be reached at 1964 Highland Drive, State College, PA 16803; phone: 814.867.9187; e-mail: soperman@psu.edu.

◢ EXECUTIVE SUMMARY

Employees in today's organizations are under mounting pressure to do more with less. Organizations face constant change in response to fierce global competition and the introduction of new technologies. As organizations scramble to outthink and outperform their competition, the very nature of work is changing. The pace of work processes has increased dramatically and has become far more knowledge intensive. Many authorities believe that *intellectual capital* (the collective knowledge of people within an organization) is key to present and future organizational competitiveness and perhaps even survival. Because of this new environment, traditional human resource development (HRD) practitioners are shifting their focus away from formal training events and toward various types of learning

◆　◆　◆

Workplace learning and performance is the integrated use of learning and other interventions for the purpose of improving individual and organizational performance.

◆　◆　◆

experiences that can solve performance problems and increase business results. The term *workplace learning* reflects the broader array of learning solutions that practitioners are now using. Today's HRD practitioners are also shifting their energies toward analyzing the root causes for gaps in productivity and finding the best solutions that will close those gaps while increasing corporate profitability. This new focus is called *improving performance*. Because more HRD practitioners are thinking about workplace learning and performance simultaneously, this is the appropriate time to describe the present and future roles, competencies, and outputs of workplace learning and performance. *Workplace learning and performance* (WLP) is the integrated use of learning and other interventions for the purpose of improving individual and organizational performance. It uses a systematic process of analyzing performance and responding to individual, group, and organizational needs. Workplace learning and performance creates positive, progressive change within organizations by balancing human, ethical, technological, and operational considerations.

Figure A demonstrates how workplace learning and performance pulls together the numerous types of interventions HRD practitioners currently use to improve human performance and blends in a clear emphasis on human learning that will sustain the organization's competitiveness through increased intellectual capital.

The following four studies depict the evolution of the training field and demonstrate an increasing emphasis on a generalist, rather than specialist, focus for practitioners. *A Study of Professional Training and Development Roles and Competencies* (Pinto & Walker, 1978) focuses on training alone. So, too, does *Models for Excellence* (McLagan & McCullough, 1983). In contrast, *Models for HRD Practice* (McLagan, 1989) takes a broader perspective that encompasses the HRD practitioner's roles in training, organization development, and career development. *ASTD Models for Human Performance Improvement* (Rothwell, 1996a), however, focuses attention broadly on what should be done to improve human performance in organizational settings. Rather than directing attention to training or workplace learning, it describes strategies for improving human performance through a variety of learning and management solutions. In 1996, the American Society for Training & Development (ASTD) initiated the workplace learning and performance competency study to assess the competencies of the field both now and in the future. This volume presents the results of this study as the ASTD models for workplace learning and performance.

Describing this emerging and dynamic field in a practical way is no small challenge. This book, however, attempts to do just that. It reflects the growing complexity and value of what workplace learning and performance practitioners must know and do.

Study Questions

This study sought to answer two significant questions:

1. What competencies do WLP practitioners, senior WLP practitioners, and line managers perceive as currently required for success in workplace learning and performance?
2. What competencies do WLP practitioners, senior WLP practitioners, and line managers perceive will be required for success in workplace learning and performance in five years?

Study Features

This study differs from previous ASTD competency studies in four major ways. The first difference is in the underlying philosophy of the study. Previous studies primarily focused on defining the field as it existed. To accomplish this, researchers began with outputs, grouped outputs by roles, and then identified the competencies needed to successfully perform the roles. Because workplace learning and performance is an emerging field,

Figure A: The WLP Wheel

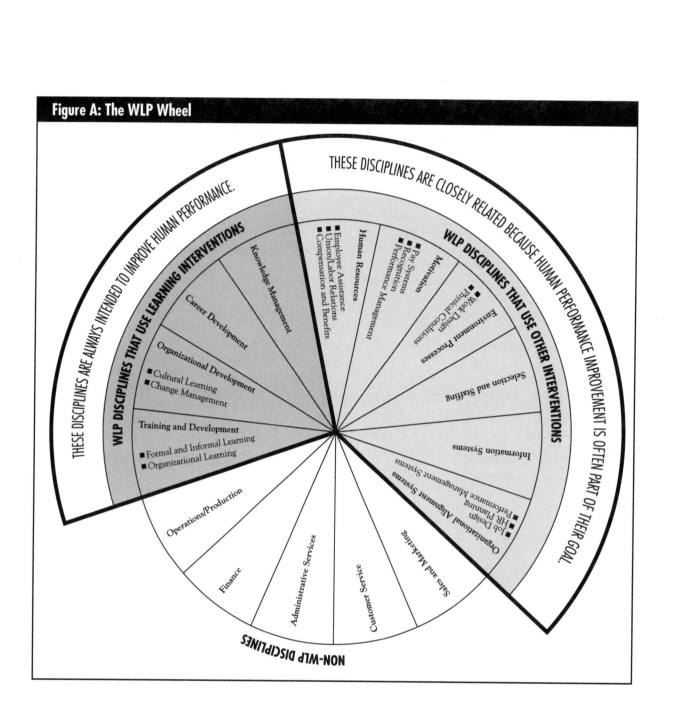

THESE DISCIPLINES ARE ALWAYS INTENDED TO IMPROVE HUMAN PERFORMANCE.

THESE DISCIPLINES ARE CLOSELY RELATED BECAUSE HUMAN PERFORMANCE IMPROVEMENT IS OFTEN PART OF THEIR GOAL.

WLP DISCIPLINES THAT USE LEARNING INTERVENTIONS

WLP DISCIPLINES THAT USE OTHER INTERVENTIONS

Knowledge Management

Career Development

Organizational Development
■ Cultural Learning
■ Change Management

Training and Development
■ Formal and Informal Learning
■ Organizational Learning

Human Resources
■ Employee Assistance
■ Union/Labor Relations
■ Compensation and Benefits

Motivation
■ Pay Systems
■ Recognition
■ Performance Management

Environment Processes
■ Work Design
■ Physical Conditions

Selection and Staffing

Information Systems

Organizational Alignment Systems
■ Job Design
■ HR Planning
■ Performance Management Systems

Operations/Production

Finance

Administrative Services

Customer Service

Sales and Marketing

NON-WLP DISCIPLINES

---

the primary focus of the present study was to assess future competencies for people who will be performing workplace learning and performance duties in the near future. The study asked respondents to rate the importance of 52 competencies associated with workplace learning and performance in terms of their importance to job success both now and in five years. Researchers subsequently grouped the competencies into roles.

The second distinction of this study is in the area of outputs. Accurately identifying a complete list of future outputs that workplace learning and performance practitioners will someday be producing is impossible. In a departure from previous approaches concerning out-

puts, this study provides sample outputs and gives guidelines for developing organizationally specific outputs.

The third area of difference for this study is in the variety of respondents who participated. To accurately define the field, this study collected input from WLP practitioners, senior-level WLP practitioners ("experts"), and line managers. Obtaining data from line managers was important because they represent both external stakeholders and the targeted consumers of the field.

The fourth difference is the primary data collection method. This study included a large-scale data collection effort through the use of the World Wide Web. Researchers downloaded participant responses directly from a Web-based questionnaire into a database. This approach mirrors the increased use of technology in organizations, and it demonstrates the impact that technology is having on data collection efforts.

Competencies

Competencies are the heart of this study. Researchers conducted a comprehensive literature review of other competency studies and related works to generate the competencies for this study. The literature review considered published works from North America, Europe, Asia, and Australia and considered all of the major topics related to workplace learning and performance. These related topics included human resources development, human resources management, instructional design, career development, career counseling, organization development, and human performance improvement. Researchers distilled the competencies out of those works, eliminated redundancies, and made refinements to reflect the nature and nomenclature of workplace learning and performance.

Researchers sorted the identified competencies into the following six competency groupings:

♦ *Analytical competencies* are associated with the creation of new understandings or methods through the synthesis of multiple ideas, processes, and data.
♦ *Technical competencies* are associated with the understanding and application of existing knowledge or processes.
♦ *Leadership competencies* are associated with influencing, enabling, or inspiring others to act.
♦ *Business competencies* are associated with the understanding of organizations as systems and of the processes, decision criteria, and issues that businesses face.
♦ *Interpersonal competencies* are associated with the understanding and application of methods that produce effective interactions between people and groups.
♦ *Technological competencies* are associated with the understanding and appropriate application of current, new, or emerging technologies.

During the data collection phase of this study, the senior practitioner group identified "creativity" as a competency important to the job success of workplace learning and performance practitioners. Researchers did not identify this competency in time for inclusion in the Web-based questionnaire.

Roles

Roles represent a grouping of competencies targeted to meet specific expectations of a job or function. Roles are not synonymous with job titles. The workplace learning and performance roles represent the evolution of the roles identified in previous ASTD competency studies such as *Models for HRD Practice* and *ASTD Models for Human Performance Improvement*. Workplace learning and performance roles are applicable to practitioners who specialize in one intervention area as well as to practitioners who take on a more consultative function by analyzing the root causes of performance gaps. The following are the seven workplace learning and performance roles:

♦ The *manager* plans, organizes, schedules, monitors, and leads the work of individuals and groups to attain desired results; facilitates the strategic plan; ensures that workplace learning and performance is aligned with organizational needs and plans; and ensures the accomplishment of the administrative requirements of the function.
♦ The *analyst* isolates and troubleshoots the causes of human performance gaps or identifies areas for human performance improvement.
♦ The *intervention selector* chooses appropriate interventions to address root causes of human performance gaps.
♦ The *intervention designer and developer* creates learning and other interventions that help to address the specific root causes of human performance gaps. Some examples of the work of the intervention designer and developer include serving as instructional designer, media specialist, materials developer, process engineer, ergonomics engineer, instructional writer, and compensation analyst.
♦ The *intervention implementor* ensures the appropriate and effective implementation of desired interventions to address the specific root causes of human performance gaps. Some examples of the work of the intervention implementor include serving as administrator, instructor, organization development practitioner, career development specialist, process redesign consultant, workspace designer, compensation specialist or facilitator.
♦ The *change leader* inspires the workforce to embrace the change, creates a direction for the change effort, helps the organization's workforce to adapt to the change, and ensures the continuous monitoring and guiding of interventions in ways consistent with stakeholders' desired results.

◆ The *evaluator* assesses the impact of the interventions and provides participants and stakeholders with information on how well the interventions were implemented and how well the interventions were received by the employees.

Outputs

As previously noted, this study treats outputs in a distinctly different way than the previous ASTD studies did. *ASTD Models for Workplace Learning and Performance* provides an opportunity for the reader to understand and develop organization-specific outputs. This process comprises the following five steps:

1. List the competencies from this study that are appropriate to the unique work and organizational culture being considered. If possible, have stakeholders determine what competencies workplace learning and performance practitioners should demonstrate in the future.
2. Determine the types of information that stakeholders feel will help the organization to meet its needs. Identify specific shortcomings of previous outputs as a basis for this step.
3. Brainstorm a list of outputs that would appropriately demonstrate each competency within your culture. (For example, survey design and development outputs might include "a valid and reliable survey questionnaire on paper or on the Web.")
4. Have stakeholders (or others who are very familiar with the organization) review and make recommendations on the list of outputs. Make sure that these outputs align with the organization's objectives and, if in a corporate setting, with the financial goals.
5. Add quality requirements to the outputs by posing the following questions:

   ◆ What are the minimum requirements for each output? Consider elements of quality, quantity, cost, time, and customer service.
   ◆ What are the desired requirements for each output?
   ◆ How may requirements change over time?
   ◆ What distinguishes exemplary outputs from average outputs?

Table A lists the sample outputs, discussed further in section four, that help to guide the reader in the creation of organization-specific outputs.

Table A: Sample Outputs of Workplace Learning and Performance Work by Role

Role	Sample Outputs
Manager: Plans, organizes, schedules, and leads the work of individuals and groups to attain desired results; facilitates the strategic plan; ensures that workplace learning and performance is aligned with organizational needs and plans; and ensures the accomplishment of the administrative requirements of the function	◆ Workplace learning and performance plans for the organization or unit ◆ Strategies that align workplace learning and performance efforts with organizational and individual needs ◆ Work plans for workplace learning and performance efforts ◆ Plans to secure the human talent to carry out workplace learning and performance efforts ◆ Objectives that support desired business results
Analyst: Isolates and troubleshoots the causes of human performance gaps or identifies areas for the improvement of human performance	◆ Analytical methods that uncover the root causes of performance gaps ◆ Results of assessment ◆ Reports to key stakeholders of individual, group, or organizational change efforts about directions of such efforts ◆ Reports to executives that highlight the relationship between human performance and financial performance

Role	Sample Outputs
Intervention Selector: Selects appropriate workplace learning and performance and nonworkplace learning and performance interventions to address root causes of human performance gaps	• Recommendations to others about selecting interventions to address or avert problems or seize opportunities • Recommendations to others about ways to combine interventions • Assessments of the expected impact of interventions • Objectives for interventions that are aligned with desired business results
Intervention Designer and Developer: Designs and develops interventions that help to address the specific root causes of human performance gaps and that effectively compliment other workplace learning and performance or nonworkplace learning and performance interventions targeted at achieving similar results	• Intervention designs • Action plans for interventions • Lists of stakeholders and participants for interventions • Links intervention design to business objectives
Intervention Implementor: Ensures the appropriate and effective implementation of desired interventions to address the specific root causes of human performance gaps in a manner that effectively compliments other workplace learning and performance or nonworkplace learning and performance interventions targeted at achieving similar results	• Plans and schedules for implementing interventions • Facilitation methods that will deliver the intervention appropriately • Consulting services • Contributions to business goals and objectives • Measurable return-on-investment
Change Leader: Inspires the workforce to embrace the change, creates a direction for the change effort, helps the organization's workforce to adapt to the change, and ensures that interventions are continuously monitored and guided in ways consistent with stakeholders' desired results	• Revised implementation plans that reflect changes in the original intervention strategy • Periodic reports to key stakeholders of interventions about their progress • Written illustrations of successful implementation cases
Evaluator: Assesses the impact of interventions and follows up on changes made, actions taken, and results achieved in order to provide participants and stakeholders with information about the effectiveness of intervention implementation	• Reports that show the evaluation results • Recommendations for future workplace learning and performance interventions • Reports that determine if intervention results caused a positive impact on business objectives

Audience

ASTD Models for Workplace Learning and Performance is for those who facilitate workplace learning and seek to improve human performance. Novices and experienced HRD practitioners alike will find this study helpful in understanding what leads to success in workplace learning and performance now and what will help to ensure that success in the next five years. Managers charged with oversight of workplace learning and performance may use this volume to take a fresh look at what they do and what they should be doing. Line managers and employees will also find *ASTD Models for Workplace Learning and Performance* useful as they assume increased responsibility for developing their careers and the careers of others and for creating work environments in which people can learn and perform successfully. Academicians will find this volume useful as a foundation for undergraduate, graduate, and certificate programs in workplace learning and performance.

Conclusions

The following recommendations, discussed in the concluding section of this volume, are based on the collected data and the experiences of the researchers and authors of this study. The following summary is a condensed version of those findings.

The Continual Evolution of Roles and Competencies

One of the greatest dangers in publishing a competency study is that the reader could get the false impression that the competencies and roles established in the study will be always applicable to the profession. At best, this is wishful thinking. At worst, this impression will lead readers into a false sense of security about their careers. The reality is that competencies and roles are moving targets. Not only do they vary tremendously by discipline, industry, and organization, but changes in the general marketplace will inevitably change the competencies and roles needed to meet this new reality. Consideration of these facts may raise the question "Why study competencies and roles?" The answer is that workplace learning and performance practitioners need to know where they have been in order to know where they are going. Although this study is future oriented, it cannot guarantee that the competencies needed for success in five years will indeed be the 52 competencies presented in this book. Though potentially overwhelming, this concept is important to grasp. Certainly these competencies can help readers to align themselves with an organization's current and future needs, but readers must maintain a critical eye when examining the changing world around them.

The Essential Basics

Traditional human resources development (HRD) activities such as competency identification, communication, and standards identification are still important to line managers. Although this competency study suggests new ways that workplace learning and performance (WLP) practitioners can add value to their organizations, they should not neglect their traditional core competencies. Workplace learning and performance practitioners need to build on their basic competencies so that they will be in a position to play a larger role in their organization's future decisions.

Learning Technologies: A Bridge to the Future

Although WLP professionals have many concerns about the effectiveness and ethics of teaching via electronic means, line managers definitely see a great potential for learning technologies. Line managers' hope that learning technologies will reduce training costs and decrease training time presents a magnificent opportunity for WLP professionals. The key is for these professionals to use electronic devices to further the learning experience, not just to lower training costs. Learning technologies represent the beginning of a learning revolution: The golden age of learning lies ahead. Learning technologies allow the tailoring of learning experiences to the individual and provide a medium that can use the Socratic method of teaching, whereas classroom instructors are lucky if they can find a way to cater to two or three learning styles simultaneously. Instruction designed for the desktop can cater to any learning style. In no way should this suggest that classroom training is going away. Classroom training will always provide an important environment for certain types of learning. Learning technologies simply provide another means for increasing learning.

The Need to Align Line Managers' and WLP Practitioners' Expectations for WLP Service

Learning to see people as vital resources is a major mind shift for some line managers, and learning to focus on business results is a major mind shift for some HRD professionals. It is pointless to debate which group requires the most education to understand how these two elements must come together for the good of the organization and the good of the employees. What is important to understand is that only through a balance of these elements can meaningful progress take place within an organization. Everyone should realize that, without people, a business is nothing, and without business results, people may lose their jobs.

Leadership: A Two-Way Street

Traditionally, HRD practitioners have provided leadership development for the top managers of the organization. In recent years, however, the idea has emerged that HRD practitioners themselves need to be organizational leaders. This idea does not suggest a corporate mutiny but an increased attempt to work with upper management in order to get them to understand the advantages that workplace learning and performance holds for the organization. Several of the line managers who responded to the survey mentioned the need for WLP professionals to "educate senior management about best practices in human resources." Although today's WLP practitioners may hesitate to think of going over someone's head to get to the root causes of a problem, doing so may be essential. WLP practitioners do not need to become corporate rebels to cause positive change, but they do need to stand by their principles, be tenacious, and creatively find ways to influence the decision makers in their organizations. Human performance theory is not mysterious: When applied correctly and monitored carefully, it will produce the results that organizations seek. WLP practitioners must take leadership roles in their organizations to put these theories into practice.

The Increasing Importance of Intellectual Capital to Organizations

Whether termed *knowledge management, intellectual capital, intellectual assets,* or *knowledge capital,* the idea that organizations must somehow capture, store, and disseminate the know-how that their employees produce is becoming vital to sustained competitiveness. As cyberspace blurs the international borders, determining where an organization's intellectual assets reside is becoming increasingly difficult. Fifteen years ago, most companies had a finite number of places where their employees worked. Today's employees are working everywhere—not only do they telecommute from their homes, but they conduct business on planes, trains, cars, and even on the ski slope. The sheer portability of knowledge and information makes organizations vulnerable to the loss of intellectual assets. Certain legal steps can prevent the transfer of organizational knowledge, but documents such as noncompete clauses between an individual and an organization rarely hold up in court. In general, the law does not allow an organization to prevent an individual from making a living. The same information that organizations want to keep proprietary is the lifeblood of an information age worker's career. Because organizations cannot "extract" knowledge from an employee who leaves an organization, they must find ways to leverage this knowledge as quickly as possible to use it to their competitive advantage. Organizations that are the quickest to use their new ideas tend to be the most successful.

Organizations today also are starting to use electronic support systems to help their employees get the information they need when they need it. These systems often require input from experts in order to function properly. This input, in turn, becomes knowledge that must be captured and stored. This need, combined with the need to protect intellectual property, makes a powerful case for an increased emphasis on knowledge management.

The Human Side of the Equation

This book's definition of workplace learning and performance includes the phrase "balancing human, ethical, technological, and operational considerations." This phrase is easy to utter but difficult to put into practice.

As WLP departments become better aligned with other business units, their supporters may be tempted to prove the value of WLP to the organization only in terms of cost savings. Although this strategy will help the WLP professional to win recognition as a strategic business partner, it could produce grave effects for the longtime viability of the organization. WLP professionals must walk a precarious line between productivity and humanistic concerns. The phrase "workplace learning and performance is . . ." holds the key to doing this. Notice that what was once two separate concepts has merged into a single entity. Rather than viewing learning and performance improvement in juxtaposition, everyone in an organization must understand that one cannot exist without the other. If an organization overemphasizes performance, it will only reap short-term benefits. If an organization sinks countless dollars into employee education without considering how this education is helping to make the employees more competitive in the future, then profitability will surely drop. If an organization assumes that a lack of employee knowledge causes all performance problems, then systemic issues such as a broken process will continue to plague the organization, and highly skilled workers will defect to competing organizations.

The Global Future

People from 28 countries participated in this study. Although the Web made this economical and efficient, the motivation behind using the technology is important. Why would people from all over the world be interested in WLP? Elaborate data are not necessary to answer this question. Work is one of the few common denominators between all people of the world. As Karl Marx pointed out in the *Communist Manifesto,* work is one of the central activities in life that give people a sense of identity. If the work experience is degrading and meaningless, a person's sense of personal worth may suffer. If the workplace provides an environment in which accomplishment and learning can flourish, however, the employee's sense of self-worth will be fostered. Workplace learning and performance will continue to be a central part of the human experience, because it represents a large part of an employee's life. As the marketplace and society become more globally oriented, the need for balancing humanistic and ethical considerations will increase exponentially. Working to find common ground with people on the other side of the world will challenge and expand everyone's social norms.

INTRODUCTION   THE EVOLUTION OF THE ASTD MODELS FOR WORKPLACE LEARNING AND PERFORMANCE

The American Society for Training & Development has sponsored five groundbreaking competency studies. The first is *A Study of Professional Training and Development Roles and Competencies* (Pinto & Walker, 1978); the second is *Models for Excellence* (McLagan & McCullough, 1983); the third is *Models for HRD Practice* (McLagan, 1989); the fourth is *ASTD Models for Human Performance Improvement* (Rothwell, 1996a); and the fifth is *ASTD Models for Learning Technologies* (Piskurich & Sanders, 1998). Each study reflects evolutionary, and often revolutionary, changes in thinking about what the field is, what its definition is, what it encompasses, and what the expectations are for practitioners and stakeholders.

The most recent study, *ASTD Models for Learning Technologies*, explores the competencies, roles, and outputs that training professionals will need to implement learning technologies within their organizations. It also provides a classification system that relates instructional methods (for example, lectures, role play, and simulations) to presentation methods (for example, computer-based training, electronic performance support systems, multimedia, and video) and distribution methods (for example, audio tape, CD-ROM, Internet, and videotape; Piskurich & Sanders, 1998). Although this work added an important understanding of the issues surrounding learning technologies, it did not intend to describe the larger field within which training resides.

In *ASTD Models for Human Performance Improvement*, (Rothwell, 1996a), Rosenberg uses a six-phase model to explore the roles, competencies, and outputs that performance consultants will need to create meaningful changes within organizations. Note that human performance improvement (HPI) is a process, not a discipline. Just as trainers use the instructional systems design (ISD) process to analyze, design, develop, deliver, and evaluate training programs, WLP practitioners use the HPI process to analyze and solve human performance problems. ISD encompasses the logical steps that a training professional can follow in order to create effective training. A host of disciplines within WLP (for example, human resources development, human resources, performance consulting, ergonomic design, and line management) carry out the HPI process. Although the title HPI practitioner does appear in some publications, it represents any person in the WLP field who is solving business problems using the HPI model. It would be far more accurate to use the term *WLP practitioner* to refer to any person in these disciplines.

To gain a better understanding of these distinctions, one must understand the preceding ASTD studies.

ASTD Models for Human Performance Improvement

- defines HPI as "the systematic process of discovering and analyzing important human performance gaps, planning for future improvements in human performance, designing and developing cost-effective and ethically-justifiable interventions to close the performance gaps, implementing the interventions, and evaluating the financial and non-financial results" (p. 79)
- lists trends in the following five key areas "that are expected to influence and change the way we work" (Brock, 1996a, p. 11): (1) performance; (2) business; (3) learning; (4) organizational structure; and (5) technology
- describes 14 terminal outputs of HPI work and 81 enabling outputs. A *terminal output* is "a final outcome directly associated with a particular role"; an *enabling output* is "a specific output associated with the demonstration of a particular competency" (p. 79)
- pinpoints 15 core and 38 supporting competencies of HPI, where *competencies* are "internal capabilities that people bring to their jobs. They may be expressed in a broad, even infinite, array of on-the-job behaviors" (p. 79)
- summarizes four roles of HPI professionals: (1) analyst; (2) intervention specialist; (3) change manager; and (4) evaluator
- identifies 16 key ethical issues affecting HPI work (Dean, 1996a).

A key point of *ASTD Models for Human Performance Improvement* is that everyone in organizational settings plays an important part in improving performance and contributes to enhanced organizational competitiveness. Practitioners, line managers, employees, and others may perform HPI work. HRD professionals are not its sole practitioners. A second key point is that no one person can play *all* the roles and master *all* the competencies described in the book. Instead, the study supplies a menu of options for doing HPI work.

The predecessor of *ASTD Models for Human Performance Improvement* is *Models for HRD Practice* (McLagan, 1989). Discussing HRD rather than HPI work, it

- defines HRD as "the integrated use of training and development, organization development, and career development to improve individual, group, and organizational effectiveness" (p. 7)
- positions HRD within the larger human resources field through the Human Resource Wheel encompassing 11 activity areas:

1. training and development
2. organization development
3. career development
4. organization/job design
5. human resources planning
6. performance management systems
7. selection and staffing
8. compensation and benefits
9. employee assistance
10. union/labor relations
11. human resources research and information systems (p. 18).

Although HRD encompasses training and development, organization development, and career development, McLagan points out that it also relates to such areas as organization/job design, human resources planning, performance management systems, and selection and staffing.

◆ lists 13 future forces affecting HRD:

1. increased pressure and capacity to measure workforce productivity, performance, cost-effectiveness, and efficiency
2. increased pressure to demonstrate the value, impact, quality, and practicality of HRD services
3. accelerated rate of change and more uncertain business environment
4. increased emphasis on customer service and expectation of quality products and services from the workforce
5. increased sophistication and variety of tools, technologies, methods, theories, and choices in HRD
6. increased diversity (demographics, values, experience) at all levels of the workforce
7. increased expectations for higher levels of judgment and flexibility in employee contribution (specifically, for creativity, risk taking, adaptation to change, and teamwork)
8. increased use of systems approaches that integrate HRD systems and technology in the workplace
9. business strategies that concentrate more human resources and require strategic HRD actions
10. changed emphasis in organizations from loyalty to merit, accountability, performance, and relevant skills
11. globalization of business, increased and expanded international markets, joint ventures, overseas ownership, and competition

12. increased need for commitment, meaningful work, and participation on the job by a larger proportion of the workforce
13. increased use of flatter, more flexible organization designs; smaller, self-contained work groups; and reduced staff (pp. 13–14).

◆ describes 74 outputs of HRD work
◆ identifies quality requirements for each output
◆ pinpoints 35 competencies for HRD
◆ summarizes 11 roles of HRD professionals:

1. researcher
2. marketer
3. organization change agent
4. needs analyst
5. program designer
6. HRD materials developer
7. instructor/facilitator
8. individual career development advisor
9. administrator
10. evaluator
11. HRD manager

◆ identifies key ethical issues affecting HRD work, including

1. maintaining appropriate confidentiality
2. saying no to inappropriate requests
3. showing respect for copyrights, sources, and intellectual property
4. ensuring truth in claims, data, and recommendations
5. balancing organizational and individual needs and interests
6. ensuring customer and user involvement, participation, and ownership
7. avoiding conflicts of interest
8. managing personal biases
9. showing respect for, interest in, and representation of individual and population differences
10. making the intervention appropriate to the customer's or user's needs
11. being sensitive to the direct and indirect effects of intervention and acting to address negative consequences
12. pricing or costing products or services fairly
13. using power appropriately (pp. 40–41).

Since the publication of *ASTD Models for Human Performance Improvement* and *Models for HRD Practice*, many HRD practitioners, line managers, and academicians have consulted them. The following soon became apparent:

- Much confusion exists about the field at present. What is it? What should it be called? Is it training? Is it HRD? Is it HPI?
- Traditional notions of HRD work are outdated. What is the new part played by those who orchestrate, facilitate, and coordinate workplace learning and performance? How is it the same as it once was? How is it different from what it once was? Where is the field headed?
- WLP practitioners cannot do everything by themselves. Professional WLP practitioners should play key roles and be accountable for what they do. However, line managers and employees must play key roles and also be accountable for results. Line managers have an obligation to create the conditions leading to a work environment conducive to learning and high performance.

Consequently, in 1997, the ASTD Board of Directors authorized a new competency study to update the society's understanding of the subject. The focus changed from HRD to WLP.

The purpose of this book is to summarize the results of the study and help readers understand what those results mean. It is not a technical report, a research report, or a how-to guidebook. It is an overview document to help WLP practitioners, managers, line managers, and employees understand the critically important, competitive edge that WLP provides. The reader should understand that this book is not a retreat from HPI or simply a new name for the HRD field. Rather, it is a reassessment of the changing roles of people within an organization (both HRD professionals and line workers) as they use the HPI process to solve performance problems. Because the HPI process uses all types of interventions to solve these problems, and because this broader array of interventions involves a variety of skill sets which go far beyond what currently exists in the HRD profession, the definition of the field also must change in order to meet this new reality.

Section one lays the foundation for this report by providing important background information. It briefly

- defines WLP
- summarizes key points about learning and performance
- reviews the origins of WLP
- provides a model of WLP

- explains the organizational scheme of the remaining sections in this volume.

Section one thus provides important information about where the field has been and how and why it is shifting to workplace learning and performance.

Section two examines trends. Recent ASTD research has pinpointed the following 10 trends that are likely to exert the most impact on workplace learning and performance:

1. Skill requirements will continue to increase in response to rapid technological change.
2. The American workforce will be significantly more educated and diverse.
3. Corporate restructuring will continue to reshape the business environment.
4. The size and composition of training departments will change dramatically.
5. Advances in technology will revolutionize training delivery.
6. Training departments will find new ways to deliver services.
7. There will be more focus on performance improvement.
8. Integrated high-performance work systems will proliferate.
9. Companies will transform into learning organizations.
10. Organizational emphasis on human performance management will accelerate (Bassi et al., 1997a).

Sections three, four, and five are the heart of this study. Section three describes how ASTD conducted the 1997–1998 study. More specifically, section three describes the questions guiding the study, reviews the study's approach, summarizes key advantages and disadvantages of the study's approach, explains the study's units of analysis, offers some important definitions, and describes the demographics of the respondents to the study. Section four summarizes workplace learning and performance roles, competencies, and outputs. Section five offers important study findings, conclusions, and recommendations.

Section six defines key terms associated with ethics, explains why ethical issues are important for those charged with WLP responsibilities, reviews ethical dilemmas stemming from steps in the WLP process model and from future forces affecting WLP, and offers five strategies for resolving ethical challenges in WLP.

Section seven lists possible uses of this study. *ASTD Models for Workplace Learning and Performance* has implications for everyone. Both learning and performance are keys to success in a dynamic world. Organizations bear an obligation to create work environments in which people can learn continuously and perform productively. As a consequence, everyone has a part to play in workplace learning and performance. The book concludes with a bibliography and a glossary.

SECTION 1   BACKGROUND

- ◆ Defining *Learning* and *Performance*

- ◆ Key Points About Learning and Performance

- ◆ Relationship Between Learning and Performance

- ◆ The Origins of WLP

- ◆ The WLP Universe

- ◆ The WLP Processes Model

- ◆ The WLP Discipline Model

- ◆ Section Summary

SECTION 2   TRENDS

SECTION 3   THE STUDY

SECTION 4   ROLES, COMPETENCIES, AND OUTPUTS

SECTION 5   RESULTS OF THE STUDY

SECTION 6   ETHICAL CHALLENGES

SECTION 7   SUGGESTED AUDIENCES AND USES

SECTION 8   CONCLUSION

Workplace learning and performance is finally coming into its own and capturing the attention it richly deserves. Many forces are drawing the attention of top managers and government policymakers to WLP. Some of these forces are

- advancing technology
- increasingly fierce global competition
- rapidly changing consumer preferences
- growing awareness of the importance of knowledge capital in maintaining a competitive advantage
- increasing individual accountability for personal learning and development.

Learning how WLP has evolved aids in understanding its importance and potential. This section describes the evolution of WLP by briefly

- defining *learning* and *performance*
- summarizing key points about learning and performance
- reviewing the origins of WLP
- providing a model of WLP.

Defining *Learning* and *Performance*

Human learning[1] and performance[2] have been the subjects of much writing in recent years. These writings provide useful definitions of *learning* and *performance*.

Definition of *Learning*

In the simplest sense, *learning* is the process of acquiring new knowledge and skills. The two forms of learning are maintenance-oriented learning and adaptive-oriented learning. Experience creates maintenance-oriented learning; this type of learning usually involves mastery of what is already known. Adaptive-oriented learning is future oriented and proactive; reflection, discovery, and innovative thinking create it. Adaptive-oriented learning usually involves generating new ideas, new approaches, and creative solutions.

Learning can occur everywhere, but workplace learning occurs in work settings. All learning is essentially oriented to the individual. However, teams, groups, and organizations can increase their collective knowledge (that is, knowledge capital), develop an experi-

---

[1] *See Brookfield, 1996; Cross, 1981; and Merriam, 1993.*
[2] *See Becker, 1977; Bolt & Rummler, 1982; Brown, 1986, 1987, 1990; Brown & Schwarz, 1998; Chevalier, 1990; Gilbert, 1988; Gilbert & Gilbert, 1989; Harbour, 1992; Harmon, 1984; Herem, 1979; Mosier, 1988; Rothwell, 1996; Rummler, 1990; and Stolovitch & Keeps, 1992.*

ence base (that is, an institutional memory), or invent new approaches for solving problems.

Definition of *Performance*

Performance is the end result of a process. A positive result is usually called a beneficial or high performance. A less positive result equates to a low or unsatisfactory performance. The objective of this book is to study effective results from productive work. Therefore, in this book the term *performance* refers to the achievement of positive results.

Among the several types of performance are human performance, machine performance, and organizational performance. *Human performance* is, of course, the result of human effort; *machine performance* is the result of machine activities; and *organizational performance* is the result of organizational activities (Rothwell, 1996b).

Key Points About Learning and Performance

Key Points About Learning

The following key points summarize the current knowledge about learning:

- Individual, group, and organizational learning can occur through unplanned or planned efforts. Unplanned learning is sometimes called incidental or informal learning (Watkins & Marsick, 1993). It is a by-product of experience. Individuals, groups, and organizations learn as a result of what they have done—that is, the mistakes they have made and the successes they have had. The fruits of collective learning experiences are stored in an institutional memory; the fruits of individual learning experiences are stored in individual memory. The goal of planned learning is the achievement of predetermined objectives intended to meet predetermined needs. Training, employee education, and employee development are examples of planned learning processes. These activities can take place in, near, or away from the work setting.
- Learning is continuous and ubiquitous. The issue is not whether learning will occur, but how well that learning will achieve beneficial results for individuals and organizations. New employees subjected to sink-or-swim experiences, for instance, eventually learn what to do. But *what* they learn may or may not be conducive to realizing individual or organizational goals.
- Learning in work settings is often problem oriented or problem driven. Few people in the workplace have the time to pursue learning for its own sake.

They are more likely to pursue learning when it helps them confront and address life and work challenges. People find time to learn when they face immediate challenges or problems requiring them to acquire new knowledge, skills, or attitudes. Those who see the practical value of learning will be motivated to learn effectively.

♦ Conditions in the organizational or external environment can help or hinder learning. Organizations, supervisors, and co-workers can support or impede learning. A learning organization creates environmental conditions that support learning. Often an organization's management has primary control over the key environmental conditions supporting learning, but everyone has a part to play in creating and maintaining that environment.

Key Points About Performance

Open systems theory is an important starting point for thinking about performance. An open system is characterized by *inputs* (such as people, capital, or information) that *processes* (such as work methods or procedures) transform into *outputs* (such as products or services). All open systems draw resources from an external environment (or *suprasystem*), receive feedback about how well outputs were received, and derive benefits from interactions with the external environment. Benefits may include profits, high returns-on-investment, or customer satisfaction. *Subsystems* are parts of organizations that contribute to the success of the system within the suprasystem.

♦ ♦ ♦

Performance is the result of an effective interaction among the resources, the process, the people, and the environment.

♦ ♦ ♦

Figure 1.1 depicts the simple components of an open system.

Organizations use open systems to create products and services. They pull raw material, information, capital, and people as inputs from the external environment. Work processes apply value-adding activities to the inputs. Organizations expel the resulting work-process outputs into the environment.

Performance is the result of an effective interaction among the resources, the process, the people, and the environment. An organization's performance is *efficient* if the organization is doing things right. An organization's performance is *effective* if the organization is doing the right things.

Taking action on any aspect of the system may improve performance. If an organization can increase the quantity or quality of inputs so that they better match the organization's needs at the beginning of the work processes, performance may improve. Similarly, if an organization can increase the quantity or quality of processes so that they better match the desired outputs, performance may improve. Performance may also improve if the quantity or quality of outputs increase to

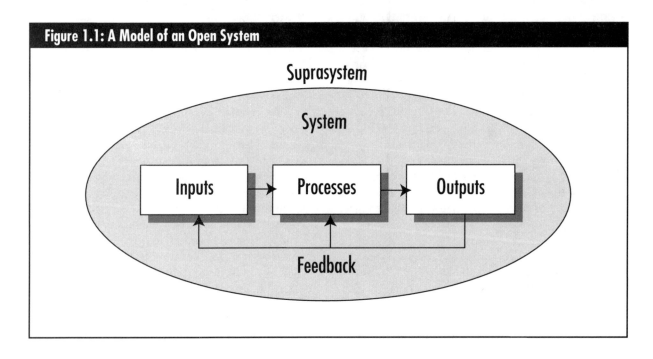

Figure 1.1: A Model of an Open System

Suprasystem

System

Inputs → Processes → Outputs

Feedback

better match what customers in the external environment desire, or if the organization increases the quality or quantity of information received from the environment to anticipate future changes in the suprasystem (which planners often do during the strategic planning process).

Relationship Between Learning and Performance

Learning and performance are intimately related. As stated earlier, performance is always an end result; it is the outcome sought from meaningful activity. Learning, however, is either a maintenance- or adaptive-oriented process directed toward achieving a result. Maintenance-oriented learning allows people to acquire requisite skills and knowledge to perform their jobs. Adaptive-oriented learning allows people to generate new ideas that can improve inputs, processes, and outputs. An example of this form of learning is a business's use of customer feedback to further improve its products. Adaptive-oriented learning may also lead to the discovery of new environments, systems, inputs, processes, outputs, and feedback methods.

Learning, then, is a key adaptive strategy for helping individuals, groups, and organizations adapt to change over time, whether that change involves becoming acclimated to existing conditions or anticipating new conditions. Without learning, performance would only happen by chance. Instead, learning transforms performance into a continuous improvement process.

The Origins of WLP

The term *WLP* represents the current evolutionary state of the field. To understand the paradigm shift that accompanies this changing terminology, one must understand how the field has evolved.

Training and Development

Training and development interventions equip individuals with the knowledge and skills they need to carry out useful work. Training is short term, geared to securing immediate benefits, and focused on results (Lawrie, 1990; Rothwell & Sredl, 1992). Development attempts to achieve long-term results and centers on using individuals as instruments for group, team, or organizational learning (Rothwell & Sredl, 1992). Since humankind first organized into societies, training has been necessary to show people how to do useful work. Development has existed in organizational settings for as long as organizations have been common contexts for work.

Although the foundations for training existed much earlier, training as we understand and practice it today

began after World War II, as a result of a number of developments (Miller, 1996). One such development was the recognition that effective training is planned training. That recognition, in turn, led to the development of such training strategies as the instructional systems design (ISD) model, first devised by the U.S. military (Carnevale et al., 1990). The ISD model, which appears in over 40 variations, provides a logical and detailed road map for developing results-oriented instruction (Rothwell & Kazanas, 1998).

Training focuses on equipping employees with new knowledge and skills. It will not, however, correct deficiencies in the workplace that result from inadequate incentives or rewards, inappropriate tools, or other barriers that fall outside the individual employee's control. Similarly, because numerous variables—including perceptions, expectations, and motivations—affect human behavior, training may not change the behavior of an entire group.

Training helps organizations meet their goals by supplying employees with knowledge and skills. When applied systematically, training uses the ISD process to solve performance problems that stem from deficiencies in knowledge or skills. Organizations will always need training that orients people to their work, upgrades their skills as work requirements change, and prepares them for advancement.

Human Resources Development

As an expansion of training and development, human resources development described a new view of employees, work, and learning in organizations. The term *human resources development* entered popular usage in 1968 after Leonard Nadler coined it in a class he was conducting at The George Washington University (Rothwell & Sredl, 1992). Human resources development is a specific extension of *human resources*—a term traced to sources earlier than Nadler (Ginzberg, 1958; Lee, 1985). Nadler originally defined *human resources development* as "an organized learning experience within a given period of time with the objective of producing the possibility of performance improvement" (Nadler, 1980; see also Frank, 1988, and Watkins, 1991). Noteworthy in that definition are the terms *learning*, *possibility*, and *performance*. As Nadler first conceptualized human resources development (HRD), it centered on the individual's process of acquiring new knowledge, skills, or attitudes (learning) to establish a basis (possibility) for improving work outcomes (performance).

Practitioners have used the term *HRD* widely, and sometimes imprecisely, despite an origin that has continually emphasized its relationship to employer-sponsored efforts to improve employee performance through learning experiences. In fact, people have used HRD to refer to

◆ government-sponsored job training programs
◆ welfare reform efforts
◆ public education at any or all levels
◆ any planned or unplanned employer-sponsored training, employee education, or employee development effort.

These associations can confuse the issue of what HRD is and what it seeks to accomplish.

In *Models for HRD Practice* (1989), Patricia McLagan points out that efforts to define HRD became complicated due to five major causes:

1. HRD was an emerging field.
2. HRD was a dynamic field.
3. HRD relied on more than one subject matter.
4. HRD existed within the larger human resource arena.
5. HRD activities were pervasive.

Despite these problems, McLagan defined *HRD* as "the integrated use of Training and Development, Organization Development, and Career Development to improve individual, group, and organizational effectiveness" (McLagan, 1989). That definition focused attention on the need to expand from applying isolated solutions, such as training, to seeking change and performance improvement. McLagan also positioned HRD within the larger context of human resource work. Using an illustration called the human resource wheel (see figure 1.2), McLagan demonstrated that HRD primarily comprises training and development, career development, and organization development, because these activities all "use development [that is, skill and knowledge development] as their primary process." McLagan also showed that disciplines such as organization/job design, human resource planning, performance management systems, and selection and staffing are closely related to HRD because "development is important [to their success], but it is not the primary orientation or process." The other human resources functions (human resources research and information systems, union/labor relations, employee assistance, compensation/benefits) are not related to HRD because they do not use skill and knowledge development as a primary tool. (Figure 1.5 presents a WLP wheel that shows the various types of disciplines within the WLP profession.)

HRD thus took an evolutionary step beyond training and development because it included organization development and career development. Organization development emerged to facilitate process and culture change and has further influenced many aspects of performance consulting. A key development was the recognition that effective cultural change requires group participation. That recognition, in turn, led to the development of the action research model. The action research model is based on the assumption that group members have the ability to identify their own problems, devise their own solutions, and establish their own action plans to implement solutions and monitor results (Rothwell et al., 1995b). The action research model provides a logical and detailed road map that assists groups in changing the nature of their work relationships.

The addition of career development to HRD was also a major step forward from a single focus on training. In the 1970s, most organizations promoted from within. A large percentage of the training budget was spent on preparing employees to be future leaders of the organization. Career development thus "focused on assuring an alignment of individual career planning and organization career-management processes to achieve an optimal match of individual and organizational needs" (McLagan 1989). It prepared employees for the future by giving them a plan for acquiring the knowledge, skills, abilities, and experiences they needed to advance within one organization. But, as employer–employee relationships have changed in the 1980s and 1990s, career development has refocused on keeping individual skills current.

HRD has helped organizations improve human performance through the use of a wider range of tools. The integration of training, organization development, and career development has led to more powerful approaches to effect individual, group, and organizational change.

Human Performance Improvement
Human performance improvement (HPI) was an important development in thinking about ways to encourage and facilitate human performance in organizations. HPI is "the systematic process of discovering and analyzing important human performance gaps, planning for future improvements in human performance, designing and developing cost-effective and ethically-justifiable interventions to close performance gaps, implementing the interventions, and evaluating the financial and non-financial results" (Rothwell, 1996a). HPI is a process, just as action research and ISD are processes. Anyone within an organization who seeks to im-

Figure 1.2: Human Resource Wheel

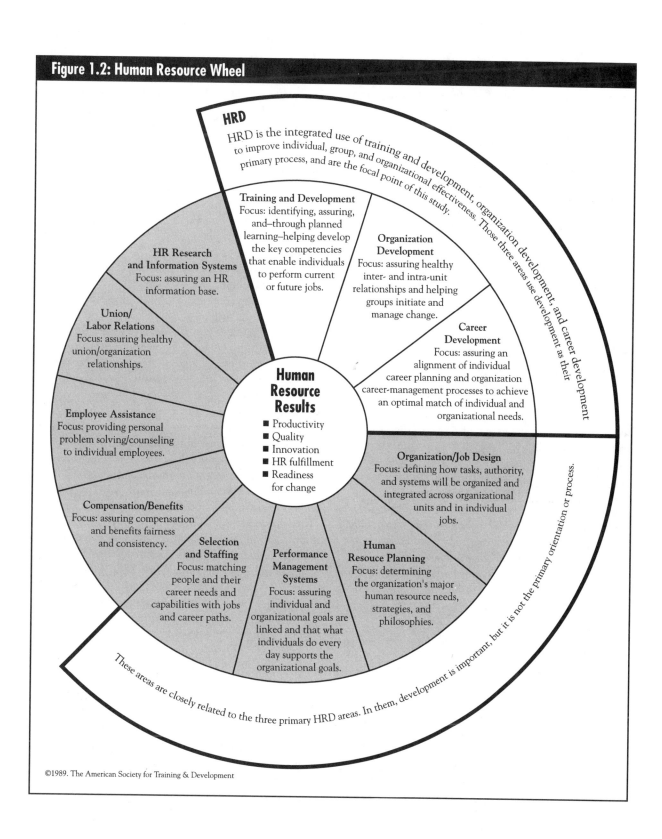

HRD
HRD is the integrated use of training and development, organization development, and career development to improve individual, group, and organizational effectiveness. Those three areas use development as their primary process, and are the focal point of this study.

Training and Development
Focus: identifying, assuring, and–through planned learning–helping develop the key competencies that enable individuals to perform current or future jobs.

Organization Development
Focus: assuring healthy inter- and intra-unit relationships and helping groups initiate and manage change.

HR Research and Information Systems
Focus: assuring an HR information base.

Career Development
Focus: assuring an alignment of individual career planning and organization career-management processes to achieve an optimal match of individual and organizational needs.

Union/Labor Relations
Focus: assuring healthy union/organization relationships.

Human Resource Results
- Productivity
- Quality
- Innovation
- HR fulfillment
- Readiness for change

Employee Assistance
Focus: providing personal problem solving/counseling to individual employees.

Organization/Job Design
Focus: defining how tasks, authority, and systems will be organized and integrated across organizational units and in individual jobs.

Compensation/Benefits
Focus: assuring compensation and benefits fairness and consistency.

Selection and Staffing
Focus: matching people and their career needs and capabilities with jobs and career paths.

Performance Management Systems
Focus: assuring individual and organizational goals are linked and that what individuals do every day supports the organizational goals.

Human Resource Planning
Focus: determining the organization's major human resource needs, strategies, and philosophies.

These areas are closely related to the three primary HRD areas. In them, development is important, but it is not the primary orientation or process.

prove human performance can use the HPI process. Although professional WLP practitioners are the most likely to introduce and advocate this process, line managers, supervisors, human resources professionals, and many others are also likely to use this model.

The HPI model encompasses the full range of interventions designed to improve performance. In a simple sense, these interventions fall into two categories: learning and management (sometimes called structural) interventions. Learning interventions focus on improving performance by equipping the workforce with better skills and knowledge. Examples of learning interventions include employee training, mentoring programs, on-the-job training, and employee development.

Management interventions focus on changing the work environment and work processes. Such interventions rely on management and employee actions to change and improve performance. Examples of management interventions include changes to the following: employee recruitment policies, employee incentive programs, reporting relationships, the layout of employee workspaces, the structure of jobs or tasks, and the way people give employee feedback as well as improvements to job-related tools and upgrades to the technology that employees use.

The WLP Field
The field has changed since McLagan offered her definition of HRD. Increasingly, attention has moved away from carrying out activities such as training and moved toward finding ways to realize results. The organizational need for increased competitiveness is driving this change in focus. Recently, many authorities on organizations have commented that intellectual capital (defined as valuable knowledge for an organization composed of human capital, structural capital, and customer capital) is increasingly a competitive edge (Edvinsson & Malone, 1997). In the words of Rosow and Hickey (1994), *intellectual capital* is "the only remaining source of competitive advantage for organizations. Most other major components of competitiveness are universally available: natural resources can be bought, capital can be borrowed and technology can be copied. Only the people in the workforce, with their skills and commitment, and how they are organized are left to make the difference between economic success and failure." In order to accomplish increased competitiveness through knowledge, practitioners have shifted their focus from activities to results, from HRD to WLP. WLP is the integrated use of learning and other interventions for the purpose of improving individual and organizational performance. It uses a systematic process of analyzing and responding to individual, group, and

organizational needs. WLP creates positive, progressive change within organizations by balancing human, ethical, technological, and operational considerations.

Table 1.1 summarizes the ways in which training and development, HRD, and WLP are similar and different.

Several operative phrases in this definition are worthy of emphasis:

◆ *Integrated use of learning and other interventions*: The word *integrated* deserves emphasis because learning and other interventions work synergistically to achieve results.
◆ *For the purpose of improving individual and organizational performance*: WLP seeks a balance between improving individual and organizational performance.
◆ *Uses a systematic process of analyzing and responding to individual, group, and organizational needs*: WLP relies on the HPI process as a systematic approach toward filling performance gaps and helping the workers to get the resources and information they need to be successful.
◆ *Creates positive, progressive change*: WLP focuses on making improvements in productivity while helping people to be successful in their jobs.
◆ *Within organizations*: WLP occurs in an organizational context. Although home and life issues also can affect an individual employee's performance, WLP interventions aim at issues that are related to the workplace.
◆ By *balancing human, ethical, technological, and operational considerations*: The principles of WLP do not condone sacrificing human or ethical considerations in pursuit of improvements in performance or productivity. Instead, WLP emphasizes these considerations at the same time that it pursues improvements in human performance and productivity.

Although WLP and HPI are closely related, they are also distinct from each other. WLP, on the one hand, is a field composed of individuals from many disciplines (for example, training, human resources, quality control, benefits management). Carrying out the broad array of interventions used to improve human performance may require specific skills such as process reengineering, office redesign, compensation and benefits management, and coaching. No single discipline could have practitioners with a variety of skills wide enough to cover all of these interventions.

HPI, on the other hand, is a process. The HPI process analyzes performance gaps, determines solutions, implements interventions, manages the change effort, and evaluates the results. WLP uses the HPI process

Table 1.1: Comparisons of Training, HRD, and WLP

Issue	Training and Development	HRD	WLP
Definition *What does the term mean?*	Through planned learning interventions, training focuses on identifying and developing key competencies that enable employees to perform their current jobs.	HRD is the integrated use of training and development, organization development, and career development to improve individual, group, and organizational effectiveness (McLagan, 1989, p. 7).	WLP is the integrated use of learning and other interventions for the purpose of improving individual and organizational performance. It uses a systematic process of analyzing and responding to individual, group, and organizational needs. WLP creates positive, progressive change within organizations by balancing human, ethical, technological, and operational considerations.
Human Nature *What assumptions exist about people?*	To be productive, people want and need to be instructed about their jobs.	People should be considered self-actualizing. Learning is key to self-actualization.	People want to learn and develop. People seek to achieve their potential. Learning and performance go hand in hand by helping organizations and employees reach their goals. An organization must strike a balance between its own goals and the goals of individual employees.
Goal *What is the major goal?*	The major goal is improved knowledge, skills, and attitudes about the job.	The major goal is the integration of training and development, organization development, and career development for the purpose of achieving improved performance through planned learning.	The major goals are • improving human performance • balancing individual and organizational needs • building knowledge capital within the organization • improving financial return.
Nature of Learning in Organizations *What principles drive learning in organizational settings?*	Learning should be focused on the job performed by the individual. The results of training should be immediate, and their relationship to the job should be readily apparent.	Increased skill and knowledge about a particular set of tasks will lead to greater organizational effectiveness. Pairing an individually focused intervention (such as training) with other interventions (such as organizational development and career development) best facilitates learning.	1. Learning interventions may—or may not—be appropriate for solving specific performance problems. The appropriate intervention depends on the root causes of the performance problem. 2. Continuous learning is an important organizational strategy because it builds the intellectual capital that is crucial to individual and organizational performance.

Table 1.1: Comparisons of Training, HRD, and WLP (continued)

Issue	Training and Development	HRD	WLP
Trainer-Trainee Relationship *What is the desirable relationship between the trainer and the trainee?*	The focus of training and development is on making people productive in their jobs. Training seeks that end with a short-term focus; development seeks the same end with a longer term focus. In training and development, the primary emphasis is on isolating the knowledge, skills, and attitudes that are essential to job success and on building individual knowledge, skills, and attitudes in line with those requirements. Consequently, the trainer-trainee relationship is akin to the teacher-student model. The teacher-trainer is responsible for teaching the student-learner what he or she must know, do, or feel to be successful in the job.	HRD adopts an integrated approach to change through planned learning. It integrates the individually focused short-term learning initiative of training with group-focused learning initiatives (organizational development) and with longer term learning initiatives (career development) intended to prepare individuals for future work requirements. Since training is not the sole focus of HRD, the relationship between trainer-trainee is more complex and varies with the type of change effort and with the results sought.	WLP does not focus exclusively on learning interventions. However, workers and stakeholders have major responsibility in planning instruction and, more important, in focusing on ways to support and encourage learning. Everyone has a role to play in that effort. The full-time WLP practitioner is a resource, enabling agent, and learning specialist who facilitates the process but does not take sole ownership of it. The learner has responsibility for taking initiative to pursue his or her own learning efforts. In WLP, the WLP practitioner and learner are partners in the learning endeavor, and both are seeking improved performance.
Means of Motivating Learning *What motivates people to learn?*	Training and development are management responsibilities because it is management's job to ensure that workers can perform their jobs properly. Employees are motivated to learn because they want to be successful in performing their jobs in keeping with management's requirements.	The integration of the following motivates learning: • individual motivation to learn the work through training • individual motivation to work effectively in groups • individual motivation to prepare for future career advancement.	Organizations sponsor learning because they are aware of the competitive importance of intellectual capital; individuals are motivated to learn in response to future career goals or present work needs, problems, or performance targets. Learning is work and performance focused rather than job focused, because jobs may go away but work seldom does.

Issue	Training and Development	HRD	WLP
Nature of the Field of Practice *What is the nature of the field?*	Training and development focus on planned learning events.	HRD focuses on the three-fold purposes of giving individuals the knowledge and skills they need to perform, helping them formulate and realize career goals, and helping them interact effectively in groups.	WLP focuses on progressive change in the workplace through learning and other performance improvement strategies or interventions.
Governing Model *What primary model best provides guidance for the field?*	Instructional systems design	Instructional systems design, the action research model, and various career development models	The HPI process model

and defines the field of people who will actively bring about these types of changes. A similar relationship exists between the field of HRD and the many processes that people in this field use, such as ISD and action research.

HRD is the field of those actively involved in training and development, organization development, and career development. Training professionals use the ISD process to analyze skill deficiencies, design and develop instructional experiences to correct the deficiencies, implement the instructional experiences, and evaluate the results. Organization development professionals use the action research process to build group consensus on a problem, find solutions to the problem, create action plans for implementing the solutions, monitor the changes as they occur, evaluate the results, and feed information back to the group. Each of the HRD disciplines can use many other processes, but the important point is the distinction between fields (for example, HRD and WLP), disciplines within fields (for example, training, organization development, and career development within HRD), and processes (for example, ISD, HPI, and action research) that the various disciplines use.

The WLP Universe

How can one conceptualize the background in which WLP is carried out? Models are useful because they help to clarify important issues by showing a complex phenomenon through an illustration. Figures 1.3 and 1.5 provide models of the WLP universe. Figure 1.3 illustrates the relationships among the various processes in WLP. Figure 1.5 shows the WLP disciplines and positions them in the broader context of a whole organization.

The WLP Processes Model

The First Circle: The HPI Process
Read figure 1.3 from the center circle outward. The center circle is the HPI process model, which is the basis for WLP. The steps in the HPI process model are

◆ performance analysis
◆ cause analysis
◆ intervention selection
◆ intervention implementation
◆ change management
◆ evaluation (Rothwell, 1996a).

WLP uses the HPI process because WLP is concerned with improving human performance and addressing individual and organizational needs. Figure 1.4 shows the HPI model in its original format, which is the same as the inner circle of the WLP model in figure 1.3.

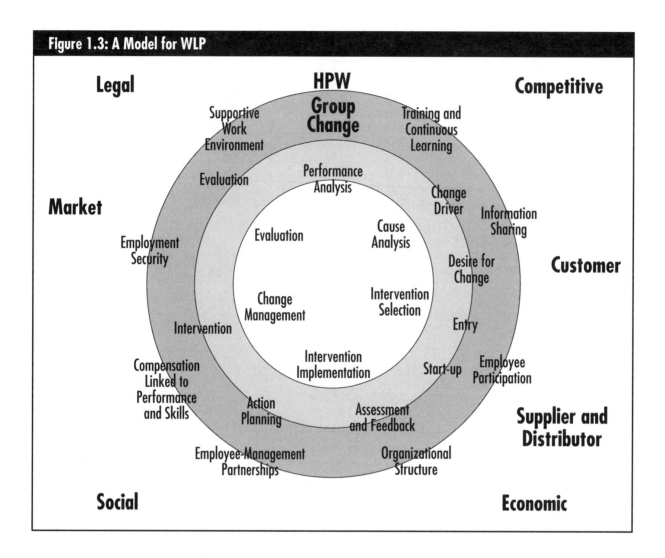

Figure 1.3: A Model for WLP

Legal · HPW · Competitive · Market · Customer · Supplier and Distributor · Social · Economic

Group Change

Supportive Work Environment · Training and Continuous Learning · Evaluation · Performance Analysis · Change Driver · Information Sharing · Employment Security · Evaluation · Cause Analysis · Desire for Change · Change Management · Intervention Selection · Entry · Intervention · Compensation Linked to Performance and Skills · Action Planning · Intervention Implementation · Assessment and Feedback · Start-up · Employee Participation · Employee-Management Partnerships · Organizational Structure

Performance analysis is the process of detecting gaps between the actual and the desired levels of performance. The gap between the two represents a need. During this phase of the process, a performance analyst compares the current level of performance to an ideal level of performance that would satisfy customers, meet quality requirements, realize organizational strategies, or meet other requirements.

Cause analysis isolates the reasons for the gap. It answers the question, "Why is this happening?" or "Why is this likely to happen in the future?" Examples of causes may include lack of skill, lack of proper equipment, lack of appropriate incentives, lack of motivation, and many other circumstances that (together or separately) result in the mismatch between the current and the ideal level of performance.

Intervention selection centers on choosing the appropriate solutions to narrow the gaps and address the causes of the gaps. Learning-oriented interventions may include training or development. These interventions can target individuals or groups. Management interventions may include changing organizational or job designs, supplying new tools, changing incentive policies, or clarifying work goals and strategies. They focus on creating an environment in which people are willing and able to perform to their full potential.

Intervention implementation is the process of applying the intervention. In a learning intervention, it refers to the process of delivering the instruction to the learner or providing the learner with his or her own means to learn. In a management intervention, it refers to the process of putting the planned change into effect.

Change management provides continuing oversight of the implementation process and helps the organization to adapt to the changes. This process solves problems impeding implementation and surmounts barriers to it.

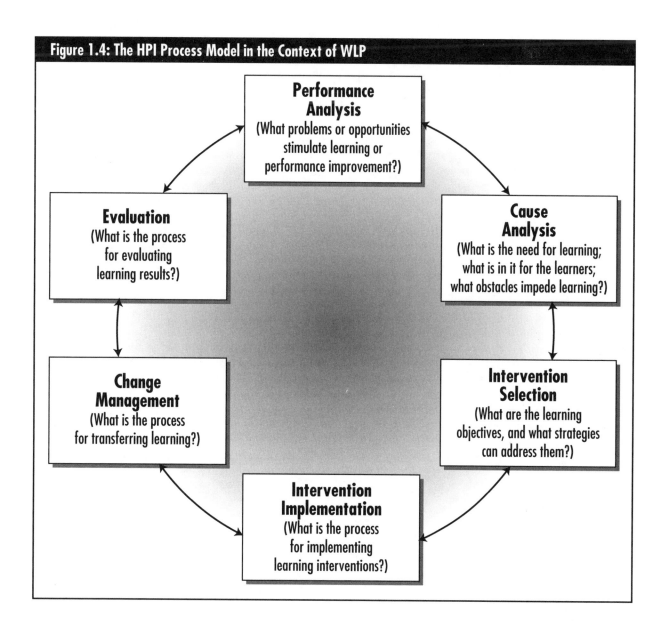

Figure 1.4: The HPI Process Model in the Context of WLP

Performance Analysis
(What problems or opportunities stimulate learning or performance improvement?)

Cause Analysis
(What is the need for learning; what is in it for the learners; what obstacles impede learning?)

Intervention Selection
(What are the learning objectives, and what strategies can address them?)

Intervention Implementation
(What is the process for implementing learning interventions?)

Change Management
(What is the process for transferring learning?)

Evaluation
(What is the process for evaluating learning results?)

Evaluation means taking stock of results and comparing how close the new level of performance is to the ideal level of performance. Evaluation answers these important questions:

- How well did the intervention narrow the gap between what is and what should be?
- How well did the intervention clarify the performance improvement objectives?
- How well did the intervention serve to meet the identified needs and achieve the desired objectives?
- What improvements in performance, if any, resulted from the intervention?
- What subsequent needs—that is, gaps between

what is and what should be—did the implementation process uncover?
- How well did the workforce accept the interventions?

When viewed from this standpoint, the HPI process model is the left brain of WLP. The HPI process must be the groundwork for all rational decisions on how to approach performance improvement. For this reason, figure 1.3 depicts the HPI process as the innermost circle.

The Second Circle: The Action Research Process
Group and organizational learning, like group and orga-

nizational change, does not occur the same way as individually oriented change or learning. The action research model is useful when thinking about how learning and performance improvement occur within groups or organizations. The second circle of the model in figure 1.3 depicts one version of the action research model (Rothwell et al., 1995b).

To solve problems or invent new ideas, people in groups usually begin with a change driver. A *change driver* is an impetus for change and a reason to learn or to improve performance. Often the impetus is a response to crisis, but it may also be a response to increased expectations of the organization's leaders. Change drivers may stem from the external environment and can include new competitive challenges, changes in customer preferences, new supplier requirements, dismal economic conditions, changing social trends, or the passage of stricter laws.

The initiation of a change effort, however, requires more than a change driver. Someone must see the need for change and convince others of that need. This person is a change sponsor: a leader with the vision, power, and resources needed to make the change. Without a change driver and a change sponsor, an organization can rarely initiate change.

When there are sufficient desire for change and sponsorship for change, the *entry* process begins. If an external consultant is necessary to the facilitation of group change, entry can mean bringing in the consultant to help lead the change effort. If an external consultant is not necessary, a change agent must step forward from within the organization. The change agent may be a member of the group initiating change or someone from outside that group. The change agent may be a human resources management specialist, a trainer, a performance consultant, or another person who can help facilitate the change effort. Line managers or supervisors may also fill this role.

During *start-up*, the change agent works with the group to become familiar with the background of the organization and the needs of the group members targeted for the change effort. For an external consultant, start-up requires preparing and negotiating a written contract for the project. Internal consultants also may prepare a written contract with the client group so as to clarify roles and emphasize necessary responsibilities.

During *assessment and feedback*, the change agent collects information from group members (individually or collectively) regarding their perceptions of the problems—or improvement opportunities—confronting the group. He or she may choose from a range of methods to collect such information. The change agent then feeds the information back to the group to help them reach agreement on the nature and causes of the problem and to build an impetus for change. The aim is to bring group members together to reach a common understanding of what the problem or opportunity is.

During *action planning*, the change agent works with the group to clarify what action should be taken to solve the problem (or seize the opportunity). The change agent's role is to help the group members reach agreement on what to do, how to do it, and when to do it. This assistance includes helping group members to establish measurable change objectives that will guide them toward the desired results.

During *intervention*, group members implement the action plan on which they agreed. The change agent helps the group members monitor progress toward their goals. The change agent periodically collects information about that progress and feeds that information back to the group members. In that way, group members stay informed of their progress and can take corrective action if the change process is on the verge of derailing.

During evaluation, the change agent summarizes progress toward the goal. Often, evaluation stimulates a new impetus for change and a new impetus to pursue learning and performance improvement. Thus, action research becomes a continuing model to guide group or organizational learning.

The Third Circle: The High-Performance Workplace Process

Individual, group, and organizational performance can only occur when organizational conditions support it. Because most factors associated with organizational learning and performance fall under management control, management bears chief responsibility for ensuring the establishment of conditions supportive of the high-performance workplace.

The high-performance workplace (HPW)[3] is the subject of much research. According to one research study, sponsored by the U.S. Department of Labor in 1995, eight key areas are linked to the HPW:

◆ *Training and continuous learning*: How much and how well does the organization support training and continuous learning?

---

[3] *See Appelbaum & Batt, 1994; and Bassi et al., 1993.*

- *Information sharing*: How much and how well does the organization share information?
- *Employee participation*: How much participation do employees have in the decisions affecting them?
- *Organizational structure*: What is the organization's structure? Who reports to whom? How effective is the structure in dealing with external environmental demands? How effective is the structure in promoting cross-functional teamwork and the sharing of expertise?
- *Employee–management partnerships*: How well do employees and managers work together in achieving organizational goals? How much evidence exists of effective partnering relationships?
- *Compensation linked to performance and skills*: Does the organization give employees and managers incentives to achieve desired results, and does the organization reward them when they achieve these results? Does the organization give incentives and rewards for learning?
- *Employment security*: How secure do employees and managers feel?
- *Supportive work environment*: How supportive of change is the work environment? How supportive of learning is the work environment? What are the physical and psychological comfort levels of employees and managers within the organization in terms of innovation, change, and risk taking?

A ninth key area not included in this study is the need to help employees adapt to change. How can employees and managers come to understand the reasons for the changes, how the changes will affect their job responsibilities, and how they can begin to see the changes as opportunities? An important point to understand about the HPW is that learning and performance improvement will not occur when organizational conditions do not support it. Establishing an HPW is everyone's responsibility.

How can one assess these conditions? One approach is to query employees and managers separately through written survey questionnaires (Dubois & Rothwell, 1996). If the organization is an HPW, then learning and performance improvement will flourish. If major discrepancies exist between the current and ideal conditions, however, then immediate action is necessary. One way to determine discrepancies is to use the survey questionnaire as an assessment and feedback tool. Subsequent improvement steps, designed to get the organization's environment on track with the HPW,

are applying the action research and HPI process models.

The External Environment That Drives the Processes

All organizations, groups, and individuals learn and perform against the backdrop of an external environment. *Environmental scanning*, the process of continuously monitoring changing conditions in the external environment, is useful in tracking the changes affecting organizational conditions, change efforts, learning, or improvement initiatives (Subermanian, 1993). Most strategic planning experts suggest that the following sectors consider the external environment:

- *The competitive sector*: Who are the competitors now? Who are likely to be competitors in the future? What changing competitive conditions stimulate learning needs or change requirements at present and in the future? What is the influence of the competitive environment on performance expectations?
- *The customer sector*: Who are the customers served by the organization now? What customers will the organization serve in the future? How satisfied are customers with the organization's products and services? What changes in customer preferences will affect the ability of the organization, groups, and individuals to perform effectively? What changes in this area will affect present and future learning needs?
- *The supplier and distributor sector*: What is the environment for suppliers and distributors at present? How does the performance of suppliers and distributors affect the organization's performance? What learning needs are evident from interactions with suppliers and distributors?
- *The economic sector*: What economic issues affect learning and performance? What changes in this area will affect the ability of the organization, groups, and individuals to perform effectively? What changes in this area will affect present and future learning needs?
- *The social sector*: What social conditions or trends affect the way the organization performs now and the way it will need to perform in the future to be effective? What learning needs do the social conditions or trends stimulate?
- *The market sector*: What markets does the organization serve now? What markets will the organization serve in the future? How do changing market condi-

tions create learning needs and affect performance expectations at present and in the future?

♦ *The legal sector*: What laws, rules, and regulations affect learning and performance? What changes in this area will affect the ability of the organization, groups, and individuals to perform effectively? What changes in this area will affect present and future learning needs?

By continuously monitoring the external environment, employees and decision makers can continuously identify needs for learning, change, and performance improvement. They also can aim efforts at maintaining internal environmental conditions so that they support the HPW.

The WLP Discipline Model

To fully understand the WLP universe, one must construct a new illustration similar to the human resource wheel. Figure 1.5 shows the range of disciplines used in WLP work and positions these disciplines within the larger context of the organization. Recall from figure 1.2 that McLagan's wheel divided the disciplines into groups: those intended to develop human knowledge and skills (labeled HRD), human resources disciplines related to the development disciplines (but not primarily concerned with skill and knowledge development), and all other human resources disciplines that bear no relationship to HRD.

The WLP wheel uses a similar methodology. It shows the disciplines that always work to improve human performance, the disciplines that sometimes work to improve human performance, and the disciplines whose primary purpose is not related to human performance. One of the reasons it is difficult to make these distinctions is that human beings staff all organizational disciplines. Therefore, one must draw a clear distinction between WLP disciplines and non-WLP disciplines. This distinction rests with the primary intent of those who work within the discipline. For instance, the primary intent of the finance discipline is to pay the organization's bills, collect money due to the organization, and perhaps invest the company's money wisely to encourage positive financial performance. Because the primary intent in the finance discipline is financial performance, finance is not a WLP discipline. If financial performance begins to erode due to a lack of human performance, however, a WLP discipline will determine the root cause of the problem and carry out an

appropriate intervention. A professional person within a certain WLP discipline may carry out this intervention, or the finance manager could attempt to solve the problem on his or her own. For instance, the finance manager may hire new employees or turn to a professional person in the staff-selection discipline. Either way, the intent of staff selection is to improve human performance.

This distinction is even trickier for those disciplines that fall in between WLP and non-WLP disciplines. For example, different endeavors that are part of the information systems disciplines may or may not aim to improve human performance. If a computer system upgrade simply makes the computer less expensive to maintain, the upgrade is a financial performance improvement. If the computer upgrade gives employees new tools and increases their productivity, it is a human performance improvement. Often this type of endeavor intends to do both. In practice, the assertion of this distinction is not necessary, but it is key to a theoretical understanding of how the HRD and performance consulting fields are expanding their roles.

The WLP field has two subgroupings of disciplines: learning and other disciplines. In the definition of WLP provided earlier in this section, these other disciplines equate to the products they provide, which are the interventions themselves. While the phrase *other disciplines* lacks specificity, it reflects the broad range of possibilities that exist when choosing interventions that do not rely on increased employee learning to improve human performance.

Not surprisingly, the other disciplines also fall under the category related to WLP. Those disciplines that focus on human learning are by default also interested in improving human performance. However, those disciplines that use nonlearning interventions may or may not intend to improve human performance. Again, upgrading a computer system is clearly not a learning intervention, but it may work to boost employee performance.

Section Summary

This section described the background of the study. It defined *learning* and *performance* and summarized key points about them. It also reviewed the origins of WLP, provided models of the WLP universe, and explained the relationship of WLP to training, HRD, human resources, and HPI.

Figure 1.5: The WLP Wheel

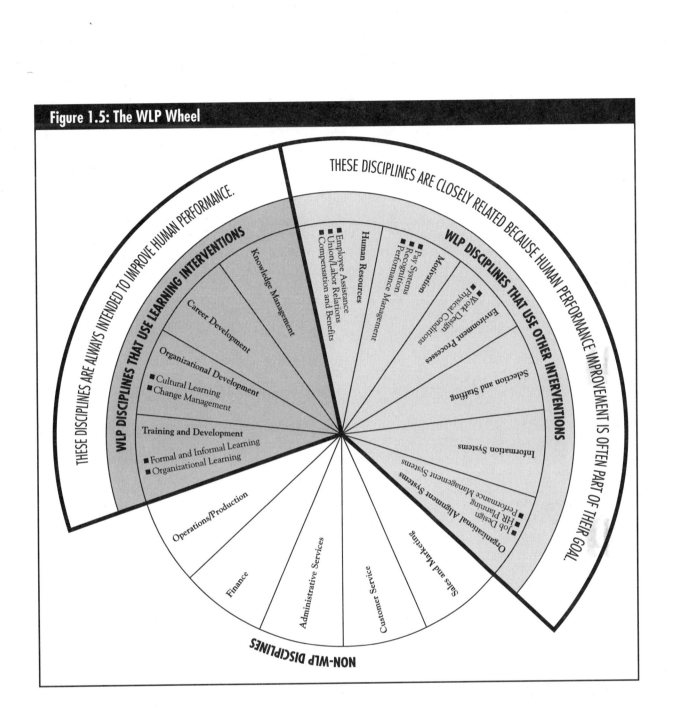

THESE DISCIPLINES ARE ALWAYS INTENDED TO IMPROVE HUMAN PERFORMANCE.

THESE DISCIPLINES ARE CLOSELY RELATED BECAUSE HUMAN PERFORMANCE IMPROVEMENT IS OFTEN PART OF THEIR GOAL.

WLP DISCIPLINES THAT USE LEARNING INTERVENTIONS

WLP DISCIPLINES THAT USE OTHER INTERVENTIONS

NON-WLP DISCIPLINES

Knowledge Management

Career Development

Organizational Development
- Cultural Learning
- Change Management

Training and Development
- Formal and Informal Learning
- Organizational Learning

Human Resources
- Employee Assistance
- Union/Labor Relations
- Compensation and Benefits

Motivation
- Pay Systems
- Recognition
- Performance Management

Environment Processes
- Work Design
- Physical Conditions

Selection and Staffing

Information Systems

Performance Management Systems
- Job Design
- HR Planning
- Performance Management Systems

Organizational Alignment Systems

Operations/Production

Finance

Administrative Services

Customer Service

Sales and Marketing

SECTION 1 BACKGROUND

SECTION 2 TRENDS

- ◆ Trend 1: Skill Requirements Will Continue to Increase in Response to Rapid Technological Change.

- ◆ Trend 2: The American Workforce Will Be Significantly More Educated and Diverse.

- ◆ Trend 3: Corporate Restructuring Will Continue to Reshape the Business Environment.

- ◆ Trend 4: The Size and Composition of Training Departments Will Change Dramatically.

- ◆ Trend 5: Advances in Technology Will Revolutionize Training Delivery.

- ◆ Trend 6: Training Departments Will Find New Ways To Deliver Services.

- ◆ Trend 7: There Will Be More Focus on Performance Improvement.

- ◆ Trend 8: Integrated High-Performance Work Systems Will Proliferate.

- ◆ Trend 9: Companies Will Transform Into Learning Organizations.

- ◆ Trend 10: Organizational Emphasis on Human Performance Management Will Accelerate.

- ◆ Section Summary

SECTION 3 THE STUDY

SECTION 4 ROLES, COMPETENCIES, AND OUTPUTS

SECTION 5 RESULTS OF THE STUDY

SECTION 6 ETHICAL CHALLENGES

SECTION 7 SUGGESTED AUDIENCES AND USES

SECTION 8 CONCLUSION

A *trend* is a recurrent phenomenon that takes place over time and gives rise to speculation on the future. A *trends analysis* examines these phenomena and often speculates on the likely impact they will have in the future. These speculations can inspire dramatic changes within organizations. In essence, trends become change drivers. Identifying the existence of a trend is relatively easy, and many studies have done just that. Predicting the consequences of a trend, however, is not always easy. (See figure 2.1.) One reason this prediction method is difficult is that any given trend can have varied effects when applied to different situations. For instance, the effects that a new piece of technology have on a given population may be quite different in the United States than they are in other nations. These same variations exist among different industries, different occupations, and different corporate cultures. A trend can also create unanticipated side effects or aftereffects. For example, the trend toward corporate downsizing has led to organizations with a smaller head count, but is has also resulted in the unexpected losses of intellectual capital and employee loyalty to organizations. Another reason that the use of trends to predict the future is difficult is that several trends can intertwine and begin to act synergistically. This combination of trends can create consequences not predictable when viewing any one trend in isolation. For example, the emergence of telecommuting is the direct result of several trends acting simultaneously in the workplace. These trends include

◆ the increased use of technology in the workplace (personal computers, fax machines, voice mail)
◆ the increased desire of organizations to save on office space costs
◆ the increased need of organizations to attract top talent (without allowing wages to skyrocket) by offering flexible work schedules.

The challenge for the WLP profession is in assessing the skills and knowledge that WLP practitioners will need in the unpredictable future. Although they may be tempted to retreat from the endeavor, the very survival of this profession requires its members continually retool themselves to meet future business challenges. Competency assessment methods must become more future focused and anticipate the characteristics necessary for high performance amid changing environmental conditions.

The American Society for Training & Development has identified 10 key trends that will affect work environments in the future:

1. Skill requirements will continue to increase in response to rapid technological change.
2. The American workforce will be significantly more educated and diverse.
3. Corporate restructuring will continue to reshape the business environment.
4. The size and composition of training departments will change dramatically.
5. Advances in technology will revolutionize training delivery.
6. Training departments will find new ways to deliver services.
7. There will be more focus on performance improvement.
8. Integrated high-performance work systems will proliferate.
9. Companies will transform into learning organizations.
10. Organizational emphasis on human performance management will accelerate (Bassi et al., 1997a).

These trends, both individually and in combination, will influence WLP in the future. This section reviews each trend, predicts possible consequences, and highlights ways that each trend may affect WLP in the future.

Trend 1: Skill Requirements Will Continue to Increase in Response to Rapid Technological Change.

The word *technology* is formed from the Greek words for skill (*teckne*) and speech (*logos*). Unfortunately, we often associate the word *technology* with gadgetry rather than with its true definition, "a practical application of knowledge" (Merriam-Webster's Collegiate Dictionary, 1996). This misunderstanding has led to huge investments in hardware and software without a clear understanding of how the integration of learning and technology can best serve the learner.

In the broadest sense, technology is a change driver. It often requires people to upgrade their skills; it creates the need for continuous learning; and it opens up new opportunities for performance improvement (Barley, 1994; National Association of Manufacturers, 1991). After all, human beings must use technology, establish and consolidate the gains wrought by technology, and interpret the results of technological applications. Organizations are beginning to recognize that helping human beings keep pace with technological advancement is crucial to their competitive success. In fact, without due appreciation for the need to help people use technology, organizations often experience a productivity paradox, which means that the

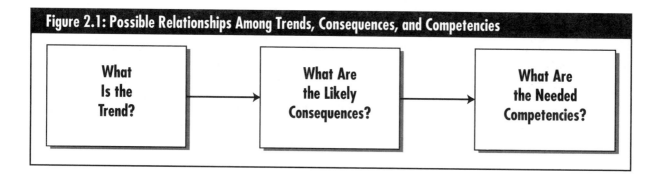

Figure 2.1: Possible Relationships Among Trends, Consequences, and Competencies

| What Is the Trend? | → | What Are the Likely Consequences? | → | What Are the Needed Competencies? |

level of productivity drops after they install new technology.

The impact of new technology on WLP will continue to be profound. The most obvious consequences will include

◆ an increased need for continuous training to help people keep pace with changes in computer technology and its applications to tools, equipment, and work processes

◆ increased research on informal, real-time learning that enables individuals to keep their skills current with advances in technology

◆ increased appreciation for the importance of sociotechnical systems (the integration of technology with human social structures) such as work teams whose members collaborate over groupware

◆ increased use of performance support systems, both manual and electronic, to help employees perform within the context of their work settings.

As a result of this trend, individuals with responsibility for WLP will find themselves at the cutting edge of these developments, challenged to keep work-related skills current. Everyone within an organization will take part in this process and will need to help solve the many performance problems created by the introduction of technology.

Trend 2: The American Workforce Will Be Significantly More Educated and Diverse.

"Increasing educational attainment" and "increasing diversity" are the key phrases to describe population patterns in the United States.[1] Addressing the issue of edu-

---

[1] *See Atwater & Niehaus, 1993; Barnum, 1991; Benveniste, 1994; Brewster & Hegewisch, 1993; Carnevale & Carnevale, 1994a and 1994b; Catten, 1993; Fullerton, 1991 and 1993; Huselid, 1993; Ornstein & Isabella, 1993; Silvestri, 1993; Strange, 1993; Wiatrowski, 1994; and Yelin & Katz, 1994.*

cational attainment, Andrea Adams of the U.S. Census Bureau writes:

Since the Bureau of the Census first collected data on educational attainment in the 1940 census, educational attainment among the American people has risen substantially. In 1940, one-fourth (24.5 percent) of all persons 25 years old and over had completed high school (or more education), and 1 in 20 (4.6 percent) had completed 4 years of high school or more, and over one-fifth (21.9 percent) had completed 4 or more years of college. The increase in educational attainment over the past half century is primarily due to the higher educational attainment of young adults, combined with the attrition of older adults who typically had less formal education. For example, the proportion of persons 25 to 29 years old who were high school graduates rose from 38.1 percent in 1940 to 86.7 percent in 1993, while for persons 65 years old and over, it increased from 13.1 to 60.3 percent. (1997, p. 1)

Educational attainment continues to increase even across gender and racial lines. "Since 1970, the college gains of young adult women have outstripped those of young adult men, until by 1993, there was no statistical difference in the proportions of men and women 25 to 29 years old with 4 or more years of college (23.4 and 23.9 percent, respectively)" (Adams, 1997, p. 1). Similarly, "blacks have made substantial progress in narrowing the educational attainment gap relative to whites" (Adams, 1997, p. 1).

Increasing diversity is also apparent from examining population trends in the United States. The U.S. Census Bureau projects that, between 1995 and 2025, "the white population, the largest of the five race/ethnic groups, is projected to be the slowest-growing among the groups" (Campbell, 1996, p. 5). The Census Bureau also makes the following projections for the same time period:

◆ Some 24 million immigrants will be added to the U.S. population.
◆ The Asian population will be the fastest growing in all regions of the United States.
◆ The Native American population, the least populous group, will grow to be the third fastest-growing population in all regions of the United States.
◆ The population of Hispanic origin will increase rapidly over the 1995 to 2025 projection period, accounting for 44 percent of the growth in the nation's population (32 million Hispanics out of a total of 72 million persons added to the nation's population). (Campbell, 1996, p. 6)

Additionally, during the same period, the "number of elderly are projected to double in 21 States" (Campbell, 1996, p. 7)—meaning that age, as well as race and ethnicity, will contribute to an increasingly diverse workforce.

Possible consequences of these changes for WLP will probably include

◆ increased attention devoted to culture-specific, gender-specific, and age-specific interventions that facilitate learning and increased human performance
◆ increased recognition of the importance of individual learning styles
◆ learning programs customized for each individual using technology to facilitate and quantify the learning experience
◆ continued awareness of, and sensitivity to, individual and group differences during planned learning experiences.

As a result of this trend in educational attainment and diversity, individuals with responsibility for WLP will find themselves challenged to customize their services to meet diverse preferences and to help organizations leverage diversity in order to create innovative products and services. At the same time, diversity will undoubtedly create some performance problems that will require the problem-solving skills of everyone working in the organization.

Trend 3: Corporate Restructuring Will Continue to Reshape the Business Environment.

Corporate restructuring refers to the de-layering, business reengineering, and process improvement of organiza-

tions. It is a process of focusing on core products or services and increasing competitiveness through decreased production costs (for example, labor costs, equipment costs, material costs).

Corporate restructuring has changed the face of America. Corporate restructuring over the past five years has eliminated at least 1.4 million white-collar professional and management positions. Restructuring has affected middle managers in particular. Though middle managers make up just 5 to 8 percent of the U.S. workforce, between 18 and 22 percent of them have felt the effects of corporate restructuring efforts.

Cost containment and downsizing are closely associated with corporate restructuring. *Cost containment* means focusing on reducing the cost of doing business while holding productivity steady or even improving it. An increasingly global marketplace and improvements in technology are two obvious causes for reductions in organizational staffing (Schechter et al., 1996). This phenomenon prompts corporate decision makers to find ways of achieving the same results with fewer resources.

The impacts of cost containment and corporate downsizing on WLP are likely to be

◆ the incorporation of informal learning into work processes as a means of improving work processes without removing employees from the work setting
◆ the exploration of new organizational structures and designs to save money by de-layering
◆ a growing use of contingent workers to reduce employee benefit costs
◆ a continued focus on demonstrating effectiveness and return-on-investment for performance improvement interventions
◆ an increased understanding of how greater human learning can improve the financial performance of organizations
◆ the revival of corporate succession planning and career development programs in order to assure a steady stream of future leaders for an organization
◆ the increased use of interventions that develop competence and intellectual capital in an organization's workforce
◆ an increased need to train contingent employees who service the organization's customers.

Corporate executives increasingly will view learning and development as important tools for containing costs and improving performance. Organizations will need to recognize that management of knowledge capital is a vital process for preserving their intellectual assets. Organizations also will need to reconcile the benefits of short-term, cost-saving measures (for example, layoffs and plant closings) with long-term costs, such as rebuilding the workforce in more prosperous times and losing proprietary information when employees leave the organization.

◆ ◆ ◆

The available evidence suggests that traditional, internal training departments will continue to shrink. At the same time, however, new functions that fall under WLP roles will dramatically increase.

◆ ◆ ◆

As a result of this trend in corporate restructuring, individuals with responsibility for WLP increasingly will find themselves planning corporate restructuring efforts. They probably will serve as members of a reorganization steering committee and will represent the process management and intellectual capital side of the productivity improvement equation. They also will help people learn new skills as restructuring efforts cause a reallocation of work.

Trend 4: The Size and Composition of Training Departments Will Change Dramatically.

One result of corporate downsizing has been that organizations have been reluctant to increase the number of staff members in training departments, despite an increased demand for training services. Many organizations have eliminated traditional training functions or outsourced them to universities, community colleges, vocational schools, consulting firms, and external training organizations. Another strategy has been to require line managers or work-team leaders to use their own expertise to train their subordinates. Although these supervisors do not hold any formal knowledge of adult education, they can offer just-in-time learning experiences that are carried out in the immediate context of the workplace setting. The fact that supervisors also hold positional power over the learners tends to be a strong extrinsic motivator. This situation also eliminates the frequent contradiction between the official process taught in the classroom and the unofficial process that often evolves in the workplace setting.

The available evidence suggests that traditional, internal training departments will continue to shrink. At the same time, however, new functions that fall under WLP roles will dramatically increase. Such roles include the analysis of human performance problems, the design and implementation of targeted interventions, and the management of intellectual capital. Consequences of this trend may include

◆ increased integration and sophistication of outsourcing partners as well as increased accountability for their results
◆ a keener awareness among executive managers, line managers, and other WLP stakeholders of the practical difficulties in making training, as an isolated strategy, effective in creating or consolidating change efforts
◆ an increased reliance on alternative training delivery systems, including learning technologies and self-study courses, to train more people using fewer resources.

As a result of this trend of diminishing training departments, individuals with responsibility for WLP increasingly will find themselves aiming learning interventions at performance problems that are specifically the result of low skill or knowledge. WLP practitioners will become more consultative, will help teams to identify their own learning needs, and will recommend several strategies for acquiring new knowledge.

Trend 5: Advances in Technology Will Revolutionize Training Delivery.

Technology will affect instruction by giving learners new methods and tools for finding and internalizing information. *Instructional technology* (the application of the scientific method to instructional design) is becoming instrumental in all phases of ISD. These phases include assessing the learner's needs, establishing instructional (and performance) objectives, designing and developing instruction, delivering instruction, and evaluating results. *Learning technologies* (electronic technologies that deliver information and facilitate the development of skills and knowledge) are likely to become more sophisticated as design techniques and technical systems improve. The following are likely consequences of this trend:

◆ An increased sophistication among stakeholders (policymakers and managers) and users (learners) about the range of instructional methods (for example, lectures, role play, and simulations), presentation methods (for example, multimedia, video, and electronic performance support systems), and distribution methods (for example, CD-ROM, the Internet, and satellite broadcasts).

- An increased expectation that organizations will apply technology to instruction, often on short notice and in real time.
- An increased willingness by learners to use the new technology and to understand its advantages and disadvantages.
- An increased sensitivity to the need to manage the environment around the users of learning technologies, without assuming that the technology will work effectively to achieve all purposes. This sensitivity will prompt a growing awareness of the importance of creating a total learning environment, which combines technology-based learning systems with social support networks that encourage collaborative learning. Also, it will prompt an increased understanding of how the technology must be transparent to the learners so that they can focus on the content. This transparency requires a deep commitment to masking the distance that inherently exists in distance learning. The new paradigm must be akin to the "reach out and touch someone" paradigm that currently exists for the telephone.
- An increased willingness to use technology to assess learners' progress and evaluate results.
- An increased need for learning professionals who also possess technological competencies, such as the ability to use, select, and manage the full array of learning technologies available.

As a result of this trend toward the use of advanced technology in training, WLP practitioners increasingly will select, manage, and use learning technologies that support learning and development. They will also require specialized competencies to change the instructional process so that it models a more immersive and Socratic type of learning. Learning retention rates must increase dramatically in order to keep up with the pace of change.

Trend 6: Training Departments Will Find New Ways to Deliver Services.

Training will continue to be an important WLP discipline. Advances in learning technologies and changing expectations about the role of trainers will allow training departments to deliver services in new and innovative ways. These ways will include high-technology approaches (for example, electronic performance support systems, or EPSS) and innovative low-technology approaches (for example, self-directed learning and group-based instruction). Trainers and other WLP professionals will lead efforts to discover new knowledge to cope with performance problems and to deliver

performance support tools directly to an employee's desktop. Trainers will continue to use the broader perspective of WLP to help maintain an organization's competitive edge by cultivating knowledge capital and making it available to all members of the organization.

The likely outcomes of this trend include

- group decision technology that captures new knowledge using the Internet or a corporate intranet
- an increased reliance on self-study and informal learning opportunities
- real-time delivery methods, including one-on-one training as well as technology-assisted learning.

As a result of this trend, trainers and other WLP practitioners will need to demonstrate proficiency in a wide range of learning opportunities and delivery mechanisms.

◆ ◆ ◆

Trainers will continue to use the broader perspective of WLP to help maintain an organization's competitive edge by cultivating knowledge capital and making it available to all members of the organization.

◆ ◆ ◆

Trend 7: There Will Be More Focus on Performance Improvement.

To realize improvements in financial performance, an organization must have a clear understanding of the human performance factors that accompany all work processes. Focusing on results, then, means devoting attention to business outcomes (that is, the monetary goals and objectives sought from a change effort), while addressing humanistic and ethical considerations. A focus on HPI means awareness of the myriad ways to improve performance in organizational settings.

A particularly effective way to focus on results is to seek goal clarity. To do this, a WLP practitioner must gain agreement from the stakeholders on the results that are being sought from the change effort. Unfortunately, stakeholders rarely agree on common goals. This causes WLP practitioners to try and perform seemingly incongruent and conflicting activities. They are torn between serving many masters with the result that they serve none. Increasingly, WLP practitioners will manage expectations (that is, what performance is expected, what customer satisfaction levels are expected, what role behaviors and results are expected, and what performance outcomes are expected) by choosing goals that are specific, quantifiable, and measurable.

An increasing focus on performance results is likely to produce an increased awareness of

- the full range of solutions applicable to the problems of achieving increased human and financial performance
- the potential gains realized by integrating several solutions to achieve positive results in human performance
- how changes in one part of an organization can affect other parts
- the organic nature of organizations (that is, the organizational life cycle of birth, growth, maturity, regression, and eventually death).

Trend 8: Integrated High-Performance Work Systems Will Proliferate.

WLP efforts do not occur in isolation. Learning and performance are heavily dependent on the environment surrounding them. Supportive workplace conditions are critically important to business success. As discussed earlier, a workplace conducive to individual and group peak performance is a *high-performance workplace* (HPW). A workplace that supports high employee involvement in decision making is a *high-involvement workplace*. These terms are related but not identical. HPW describes an end result (that is, an organization that is outperforming its competitors). High-involvement workplaces can lead to such a condition, but employee participation in decisions is only one of several factors that lead to overall success. WLP requires employee participation at many levels of the organization. Within any successful change effort, all of the following individuals and groups must be part of the solution:

- *change agents:* people who monitor the change process and help the organization adapt to the change
- *change advocates:* people who support the change but lack the power and resources to make it happen
- *change sponsors:* people who support the change and have the power and resources to make it happen
- *change implementors:* business unit leaders who enact the changes within their departments
- *change targets:* the groups of people whom the changes most directly affect.

Although the resources and positional power of these five groups vary, the need to secure their commitment and acceptance for the proposed interventions is critical. Without that sense of ownership for the change, any one of these groups can become a change killer.

To sustain high-performance and high-involvement organizations, WLP practitioners need to

- isolate, measure, and maintain effective organizational conditions that are conducive to learning and performance
- guide managers toward practices that nurture performance and learning
- link WLP efforts to organizational strategies and core competencies. The results of this trend are likely to be the same as those identified in trend seven.

Trend 9: Companies Will Transform Into Learning Organizations.

Since the publishing of Peter Senge's book *The Fifth Discipline* in 1990, corporate executives have desperately searched for a model organization that exemplifies a learning organization. Of course, their interest in this phenomenon exceeds mere curiosity. The basic premise that intrigues enlightened corporate executives is that a "smarter" organization is a more profitable organization. The trouble has been in finding a true learning organization and then trying to copy the complex behaviors that create this condition.

Perhaps one of the elements that has been missing in this quest is a comprehensive understanding of the link between learning and performance. For example, if an organization attempts to become a learning organization strictly by increasing course offerings, it is likely to fail.

A true learning organization encourages and nurtures learning at the very core of each and every work process. In the simplest sense, a learning organization is one in which individuals and groups are continuously improving their abilities to learn and perform. It grows intellectually through its individual and collective membership.

Developing a learning organization involves building intellectual capital and using knowledge management. *Intellectual capital* is a phrase that refers to the collective economic value of an organization's workforce, which stems from its experience, knowledge, and know-how.[2] As organizations begin to quantify their strategic strengths, awareness of the importance of knowledge capital and of organizational learning is growing. The interesting part of this movement is that organizations are attempting to capture and use organizational knowledge while downsizing and outsourcing. Although downsizing strategies may reduce operating costs in the short term, they often erode the organization's resources of human talent over time.

The emergence of true learning organizations likely will require

- sophisticated plans for developing, integrating, and aligning human talent with organizational goals
- the ability to assess and measure the value and competitiveness of their knowledge capital
- the ability to monitor closely the effects of new company policies on the internal learning environment
- an increased need for intrinsic motivational systems that make knowledge workers want to keep contributing to their current organization
- better intellectual property protection for proprietary information that the organization develops.

To help their organizations address these needs, WLP practitioners need to

- encourage team learning, because many learning projects and many performance improvement efforts occur in a group setting
- establish shared visions so that people see the need for learning
- build faster communication channels and collaborative communication systems so people can share what they learn
- maintain a vibrant and efficient infrastructure that nurtures, supports, encourages, and rewards creative thinking that leads to increased performance and competitiveness.

Trend 10: Organizational Emphasis on Human Performance Management Will Accelerate.

Organizations are discovering that individuals rarely achieve meaningful results on their own. As a result, they are moving to the use of team-based structures. As discussed in trend three, the era of the middle manager is over. In general, cross-functional teams are performing the responsibilities of planning work, monitoring progress, appraising performance, hiring and firing, and acquiring resources. Not only do teams lower the

---

2 *See Brooking, 1996; Edvinsson & Malone, 1997; Nonaka & Takeuchi, 1995; Stewart, 1997; and Sveiby, 1997.*

◆ ◆ ◆

Not only do teams lower the overall payroll, but they also secure a sense of loyalty and commitment to certain projects that is unprecedented in traditional corporate hierarchies.

◆ ◆ ◆

overall payroll, but they also secure a sense of loyalty and commitment to certain projects that is unprecedented in traditional corporate hierarchies. Although the term *empowerment* has become a cliché in some circles, it does embody the idea of corporate democracy.

These same democratic principles apply to WLP activities. Organizations cannot delegate responsibility for learning and performance to one department or function. Instead, everyone shares responsibility for linking individual and organizational improvement. WLP practitioners, employees, managers, and executives must establish contemporary understandings of the part they play in this new relationship.

Performance management is a continuing effort conducted proactively. It informs people of performance goals, recommends ways to achieve those goals, supplies incentives and rewards for performance, and offers ways to define and measure success. Performance management is closely linked to the idea of establishing and maintaining HPWs and learning organizations. Performance management is the means to achieve the results. Managers, employees, and other stakeholders carry out performance management in real time.

Applying performance management theory within an organization probably will require WLP practitioners to

- establish performance targets and clarify work and performance expectations
- communicate those expectations to the entire organization on a continuing basis
- find better ways to provide faster, more specific feedback to performers
- provide desirable incentives so that people want to perform and tie meaningful rewards to goals so that people want to achieve the desired results.

Of the 10 trends above, trends four, five, six, and seven will be especially influential in shaping the landscape of WLP (Bassi et al., 1997b). They are the most prevalent and rapidly expanding trends, and combined they represent a paradigm shift that has the potential to forever change the face of corporate education. If training departments become smaller (trend four), the use of alternative delivery methods and learning methods (trends five and six) will no doubt accelerate. As technology becomes cheaper, better, and more accessible, learners will come to expect just-in-time training (trend five). As organizations free corporate trainers from some of the more fruitless tasks (for example, offering training for a structural problem) and mundane activities (for example, scheduling rooms and grading tests), the corporate trainers can retool themselves to add value to the organization in other ways. The most direct way for them to add this value is to begin

applying the principles and procedures outlined in the HPI model (trend seven).

Section Summary

A *trend* is a recurrent phenomenon that takes place over time and gives rise to speculation on the future. A *trends analysis* examines these phenomena and often speculates on the likely impact they will have in the future. Identifying the existence of a trend is often relatively easy, but predicting the consequences of a trend is more difficult. This section reviewed 10 key trends that ASTD has identified as having a potentially significant influence on the field of WLP in the future.

This section describes the questions guiding the study, reviews its approach, summarizes the key advantages and disadvantages of its methodology, explains its units of analysis, and offers some important definitions. This section also describes the demographics of the respondent population.

Questions Guiding the Study

This study sought answers to the following questions:

1. What competencies do WLP practitioners, senior WLP practitioners, and line managers perceive as *currently* required for success in WLP?
2. What competencies do WLP practitioners, senior WLP practitioners, and line managers perceive *will be required* for success in WLP in five years?

The Study's Approach

As shown in figure 3.1, the researchers conducted this study in eight distinct phases.

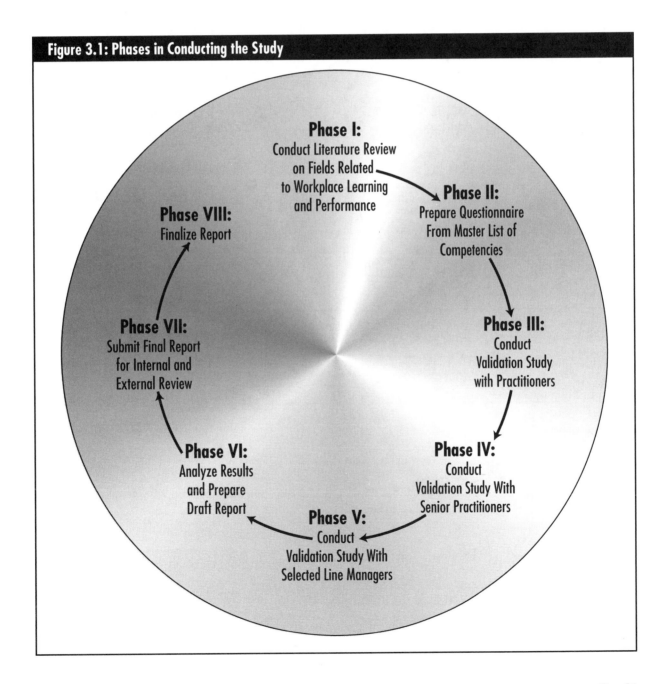

Figure 3.1: Phases in Conducting the Study

Phase I:
Conduct Literature Review on Fields Related to Workplace Learning and Performance

Phase II:
Prepare Questionnaire From Master List of Competencies

Phase III:
Conduct Validation Study with Practitioners

Phase IV:
Conduct Validation Study With Senior Practitioners

Phase V:
Conduct Validation Study With Selected Line Managers

Phase VI:
Analyze Results and Prepare Draft Report

Phase VII:
Submit Final Report for Internal and External Review

Phase VIII:
Finalize Report

In Phase I, the researchers conducted a comprehensive literature review in the United States and other nations on WLP-related competency studies in such fields as HRD, human resource management, instructional design, career development, career counseling, organization development, and HPI.[1]

---

[1] *See Brethower, 1995; Cameron, 1988; Competency Standards Body—Assessors & Workplace Trainers, 1994; Dixon et al., 1995; Eubanks et al., 1990; Foshay et al., 1986; Foshay et al., 1990; Gayeski, 1995; Ginkel et al., 1994; Hutchison et al., 1988; Leach, 1991; Lee, 1994; Lippitt & Nadler, 1967; McLagan, 1989; McLagan & McCullough, 1983;. Marquardt & Engel, 1993a, 1993b; Nadler, 1962; Pinto & Walker, 1978; Rae, 1993; Rijk et al., 1994; Rothwell et al., 1995a; and Stolovich et al., 1995; Training and Development Lead Body, 1992; and Ulrich et al., 1989.*

In Phase II, the researchers prepared a questionnaire from the master list of competencies. The data collection took two forms: a paper-based questionnaire for the line managers and experts, and an electronic form on ASTD's World Wide Web site (www.astd.org) for the practitioner group. In both instances, the questionnaire asked respondents to rate how important each of the 52 competencies are for an individual who performs WLP work. They rated each competency 1 to 5 ("1" being not important and "5" being extremely important) on its current importance and its importance in five years. Figure 3.2 shows a sample of the questionnaire. The questionnaire asked for demographic information—including age, gender, ethnic background, years of work experience, and professional discipline—from all three respondent groups. The demographics discussion later in this section provides this information.

Figure 3.2: Sample of the Questionnaire

Competency Survey

Please rate how important you consider each of the following competencies for an individual at your current level, and at the next higher level to that which you currently hold. Please use the following rating scale for your responses:

1=Not Important   2=Slightly Important   3=Important   4=Very Important   5=Extremely Important

	Now					In Five Years				
	N	S	I	V	E	N	S	I	V	E
Performance Gap Analysis: performing "front-end analysis" by comparing actual and ideal performance levels in the workplace. Identifying opportunities and strategies for performance improvement.	1	2	3	4	5	1	2	3	4	5
Survey Design and Development: creating survey approaches that use open-ended (essay) and closed style questions (multiple choice and Likert items) for collecting data. Preparing instruments in written, verbal, or electronic formats.	1	2	3	4	5	1	2	3	4	5
Analytical Thinking: clarifying complex issues by breaking them down into meaningful components and synthesizing related items.	1	2	3	4	5	1	2	3	4	5
Competency Identification: identifying the skills, knowledge, and attitudes required to perform work.	1	2	3	4	5	1	2	3	4	5

The researchers conducted the Web-based data collection effort from May 1997 through the end of September 1997. In order to increase the response rate of the Web-based questionnaire, ASTD advertised it in publications and at their conferences. During this phase, the researchers also identified senior WLP practitioners who met predetermined criteria for participation in Phase III.

In Phase III, the researchers sent a paper copy of a nearly identical data collection instrument to a carefully selected group of senior WLP practitioners. In addition to rating the importance of the competencies provided, this group answered the following qualitative questions:

◆ "Do you believe that the competencies listed above accurately represent those critical to the job success of workplace learning and performance professionals? Why or why not?"
◆ "Please identify any specific competencies critical to the job success of workplace learning and performance professionals, either now or in the future, which are not listed above."
◆ "Please identify what you consider to be the significant future trends which will most profoundly affect the role and/or job success of workplace learning and performance professionals over the next five years."

◆ "What do you foresee as the primary role(s) of workplace learning and performance over the next five years. Why?

On the basis of predetermined criteria (see figure 3.3), the researchers selected 65 senior WLP practitioners. Of the 65, 50 (76.9 percent) responded to the survey. These respondents, who collectively composed an external advisory review panel, are listed in the acknowledgments to this book. Members of this group had time during July and August 1997 to complete and return the questionnaire. To permit subsequent comparisons, the researchers kept these responses separate from the responses of other WLP practitioners.

In Phase IV, the researchers transmitted the same data collection instrument in paper copy to 31 selected line managers from various organizations. These line managers met criteria for line management comparable to, but not identical to, those established for senior WLP practitioners. (See figure 3.4 for the criteria.) The line managers had one month to complete and return the survey. As in Phase III, the researchers kept these responses separate from the responses of the other two groups to permit subsequent comparisons.

In Phase V, the researchers asked the members of the senior WLP practitioner group who had responded to the initial survey to rate each competency's impor-

---

Figure 3.3: Criteria for Selecting Participants for the External Advisory Review Panel

To be eligible for the external advisory panel, participants had to meet the following criteria:

A. Demonstrated commitment to the knowledge and practice of the WLP field—including evidence of nationally/internationally recognized publications, development and advancement of theories within WLP institutions, and development of major established project(s) in WLP. Additional evidence includes:
   ◆ Major projects developed by the individual and the objectives and outcomes of each
   ◆ Theories developed by the individual and information on how they have been utilized
   ◆ Published and distributed articles, books, videos, and programs
   ◆ A minimum of 15 years of work experience in the WLP field or a related field
   ◆ A minimum of 10 years of work experience in managing WLP initiatives

B. Evidence of influence on other WLP professionals. This evidence includes
   ◆ Participation/contribution to professional societies
   ◆ Utilization of theories and practices

C. Evidence of national or international acclaim for work in the WLP field. This evidence includes
   ◆ Receipt of awards and honorary degrees
   ◆ Major speaking engagements
   ◆ Appearances in films, videos, or TV programs related to WLP.

Figure 3.4: Criteria for Line Management Participants

To be eligible for the external advisory review panel, line management participants had to meet the following criteria:

A. Involvement with WLP practitioners at least one time per month on average

B. Over six years of management experience

C. Over ten years of professional experience

D. Work in one of the six following fields (or a related field):
- Administrative services
- Customer service
- Finance
- Information services/information technology
- Sales/marketing
- Operations/Production/Manufacturing.

E. Employment in one of the following types of businesses:
- Manufacturing
- Communications
- Consulting
- Education
- Health care
- Finance, insurance, or real estate
- Retail trade
- Transportation
- Utilities
- Service.

tance to success in each of the seven WLP roles. Of the 50 asked, 24 (48 percent) responded.

In Phase VI, the researchers analyzed the study results and compared the three studies. They noted points of agreement and disagreement about the current and future WLP competencies among WLP practitioners, senior WLP practitioners, and line managers. They then finalized the results of this analysis in a draft report.

In Phase VII, the researchers submitted the draft report, with its conclusions, to the ASTD internal advisory review panel. That panel then evaluated all sections of the final report. As a final step in validating the study, several members of the external advisory review panel reviewed the study's major findings and made recommendations. In Phase VIII, the final phase, the researchers reviewed the suggestions made by the internal and external advisory review panels and made stylistic changes to clarify the report.

Advantages and Disadvantages of the Study's Approach

The study's approach had numerous advantages and disadvantages worthy of note. One advantage of this competency study was that it used the first Web-based data collection effort ever applied to this field. The study revealed that new technology can be a powerful tool for collecting information from many individuals who are scattered around the world. This technology opens new opportunities for subsequent research in the WLP field. Additionally, collection of data via the World Wide Web eliminated data-entry and processing errors during the analysis phases. Respondents entered data in a form that researchers subsequently transferred directly into the database, eliminating the possibility of introducing errors during data entry—a common problem confronting survey researchers.

A second advantage of the study was that it used a threefold validation process. It was not an "expert study" alone because WLP practitioners and selected line managers also participated. Instead, the validation process for the study provided a basis for a limited assessment of how key constituency groups view the importance of various present and future WLP competencies. This study compares WLP practitioners' perceptions about competencies with other groups' perceptions.

However, several limitations also characterized the study's approach. For instance, the study was limited to the opinions of those participating in it. One cannot generalize the results to represent the view of *all* WLP practitioners. A second disadvantage was that, as is the case for many written questionnaire studies, the researchers could not easily verify the experience levels and expertise of the respondents. However, by requiring a two-step entry process to the Web site and double-checking the database when individuals did not match the computerized ASTD membership list, the researchers did make an effort to verify that respondents were who they said they were. They verified the name and membership number of each respondent who reported being an ASTD member.

A third disadvantage was that participation on the Web site required current technology (that is, a relatively recent version of an appropriate version of browser software). The use of older, outdated software was the cause of a vast majority of difficulties experienced by respondents trying to access the Web-based questionnaire.

A fourth limitation, perhaps the most significant, was in the uneven number of responses from various disciplines and levels. The overall number of responses was high, as was the number of responses in the disciplines of training and organization development. However, the number of responses in the career development, management development, human resources management, and generalist disciplines was not sufficiently large to allow for meaningful findings by level within these disciplines.

Who Participated in the Study?

Three distinct target groups participated in this competency study: WLP practitioners (anyone who could access the Web-based questionnaire), senior WLP practitioners (the external advisory review panel), and line managers (leaders of non-WLP business units). The WLP practitioner group was particularly diverse, with respondents from entry to executive levels. The comparison of their different perspectives provides unique and applicable insights into the nature of the field both now and five years into the future.

The demographics serve to describe the participants and provide a frame of reference for the study's findings. During the large-scale data collection phase of this study, 1,254 individuals completed the log-in procedure and some part of the Web-based assessment instrument. Of these 1,254 respondents, 1,031 (82.2 percent) completed the entire survey. Researchers sent e-mail follow-ups on three separate occasions to all respondents who had completed the demographic section but who had not completed the survey. As a feature of the survey design, individuals could log in and resume filling out the survey where they had previously left off. More than 50 individuals who received the follow-ups took advantage of this feature and completed the survey.

Interestingly, the key demographics of the 1,031 WLP practitioners who participated in this study approximate the key demographics of the *ASTD National Members Report*, based on surveys as of February 28, 1997.

Demographics

WLP Practitioner Group
Respondents to the large-scale competency assessment survey represented 28 countries in Africa, Asia, Australia, the Middle East, Central America, North America, and South America. Of the 1,031 respondents, 230 (22.3 percent) reported they were not members of ASTD. Analysis revealed no statistical difference between nonmember and member response results; therefore, the researchers combined data from all respondents and included them in this study.

In terms of race demographics, 840 (81.5 percent) of the respondents were white, 85 (8.2 percent) were Asian, 39 (3.8 percent) were black, and the remaining 67 (6.5 percent) comprised individuals of Arab, Indian, Latino/Hispanic, or Native American background. Of the 1,031 respondents, 619 (60.0 percent) were female

◆　◆　◆

Three distinct target groups participated in this competency study: WLP practitioners (anyone who could access the Web-based questionnaire), senior WLP practitioners (the external advisory review panel), and line managers (leaders of non-WLP business units).

◆　◆　◆

and 412 (40.0 percent) were male. The average age of the respondents was 41.7 years old.

The average respondent had 11 to 15 years of professional experience and six to 10 years of experience in fields related to WLP. An overwhelming majority of respondents (989, or 95.9 percent) reported having earned some level of college degree. Three hundred seventy respondents (35.9 percent) reported having a bachelor's degree, and 476 (46.2 percent) reported having a master's degree.

Respondents represented 13 types of businesses, with the primary areas being manufacturing (185 respondents, or 17.9 percent), consulting (178 respondents, 17.3 percent), and education (124 respondents, 12.0 percent). (See figure 3.5.) The respondents represented organizations of varying sizes: 237 respondents (23.0 percent) came from small businesses, those with fewer than 100 employees, 187 respondents (19.0 percent) came from medium-sized entities, with 100 to 499 employees, and 607 respondents (58.0 percent) came from organizations with greater than 500 employees. (See figure 3.6.)

The respondents' primary WLP disciplines and the current levels within their organizations are of foremost significance to this study and to the use of the findings. The questionnaire asked the respondents to report their primary discipline: 572 (55.5 percent) reported

training; 167 (16.2 percent) reported organization development; 93 (9.0 percent) reported generalist; 88 (8.5 percent) reported management development; 77 (7.5 percent) reported human resource management; and 34 (3.3 percent) reported career development. (See figure 3.7.) In terms of current level within the organization, 68 (6.6 percent) reported being at the executive level; 350 (33.9 percent) reported being at the managerial level; 160 (15.5 percent) reported being at the supervisory level; 317 (30.7 percent) reported being at entry level; and 136 (13.2 percent) reported being private consultants or self-employed. (See figure 3.8.)

Expert Group
Figures 3.9 through 3.12 give some of the primary demographic statistics of the 50 expert group members. Figures 3.13 through 3.16 give some of the primary demographic statistics of the 23 line manager group members.

Section Summary
This section described the questions guiding the study, reviewed the study's approach, summarized key advantages and disadvantages of the study's approach, explained the study's units of analysis, offered some important definitions, and reviewed the demographics of the study respondents.

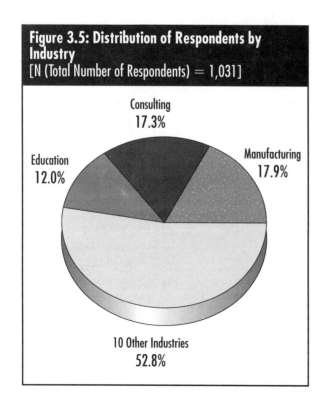

Figure 3.5: Distribution of Respondents by Industry
[N (Total Number of Respondents) = 1,031]

Consulting 17.3%

Education 12.0%

Manufacturing 17.9%

10 Other Industries 52.8%

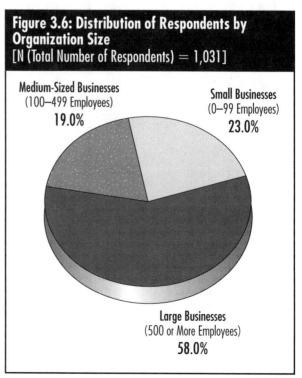

Figure 3.6: Distribution of Respondents by Organization Size
[N (Total Number of Respondents) = 1,031]

Medium-Sized Businesses (100–499 Employees) 19.0%

Small Businesses (0–99 Employees) 23.0%

Large Businesses (500 or More Employees) 58.0%

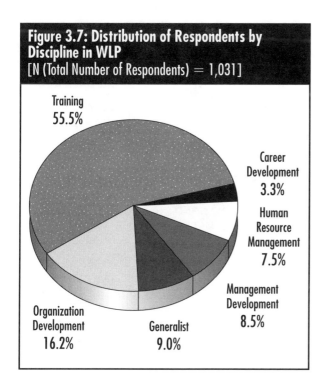

Figure 3.7: Distribution of Respondents by Discipline in WLP
[N (Total Number of Respondents) = 1,031]

Training 55.5%

Career Development 3.3%

Human Resource Management 7.5%

Management Development 8.5%

Generalist 9.0%

Organization Development 16.2%

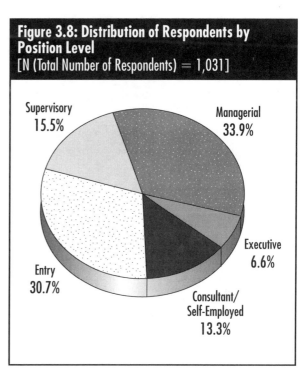

Figure 3.8: Distribution of Respondents by Position Level
[N (Total Number of Respondents) = 1,031]

Supervisory 15.5%

Managerial 33.9%

Executive 6.6%

Consultant/ Self-Employed 13.3%

Entry 30.7%

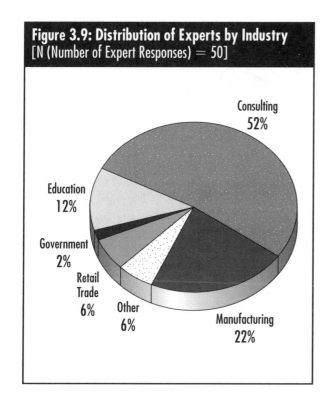

Figure 3.9: Distribution of Experts by Industry
[N (Number of Expert Responses) = 50]

Consulting 52%

Education 12%

Government 2%

Retail Trade 6%

Other 6%

Manufacturing 22%

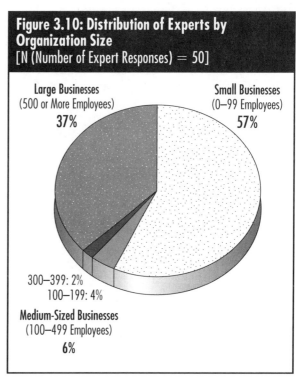

Figure 3.10: Distribution of Experts by Organization Size
[N (Number of Expert Responses) = 50]

Large Businesses (500 or More Employees) 37%

Small Businesses (0–99 Employees) 57%

300–399: 2%
100–199: 4%

Medium-Sized Businesses (100–499 Employees) 6%

Figure 3.11: Distribution of Experts by WLP Discipline
[N (Number of Expert Responses) = 50]

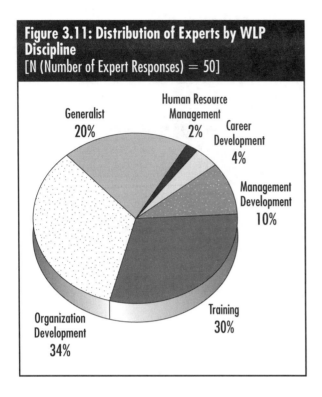

Generalist 20%

Human Resource Management 2%

Career Development 4%

Management Development 10%

Training 30%

Organization Development 34%

Figure 3.12: Distribution of Experts by Position Level
[N (Number of Expert Responses) = 50]

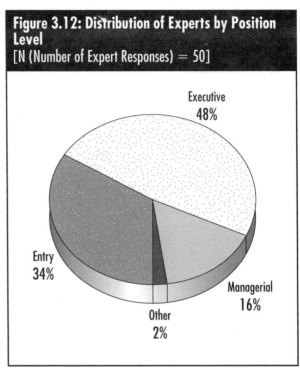

Executive 48%

Entry 34%

Other 2%

Managerial 16%

Figure 3.13: Distribution of Line Managers by Industry
[N (Number of Line Manager Respondents) = 23]

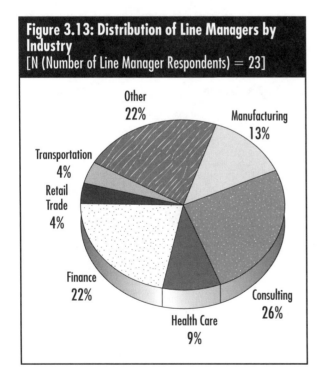

Other 22%

Manufacturing 13%

Transportation 4%

Retail Trade 4%

Finance 22%

Health Care 9%

Consulting 26%

Figure 3.14: Distribution of Line Managers by Organization Size
[N (Number of Line Manager Respondents) = 23]

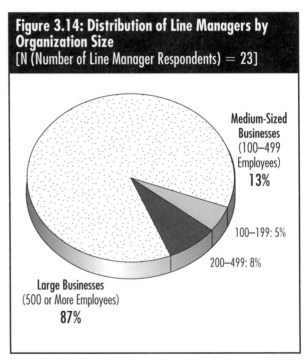

Medium-Sized Businesses (100–499 Employees) 13%

100–199: 5%

200–499: 8%

Large Businesses (500 or More Employees) 87%

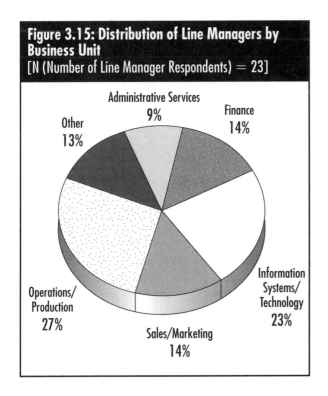

Figure 3.15: Distribution of Line Managers by Business Unit
[N (Number of Line Manager Respondents) = 23]

Administrative Services 9%
Finance 14%
Other 13%
Operations/ Production 27%
Sales/Marketing 14%
Information Systems/ Technology 23%

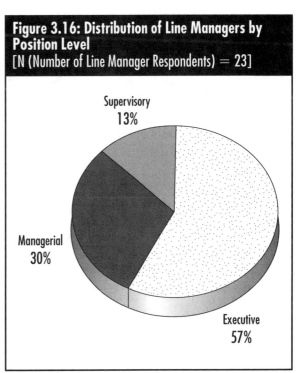

Figure 3.16: Distribution of Line Managers by Position Level
[N (Number of Line Manager Respondents) = 23]

Supervisory 13%
Managerial 30%
Executive 57%

SECTION 1 BACKGROUND

SECTION 2 TRENDS

SECTION 3 THE STUDY

SECTION 4 ROLES, COMPETENCIES, AND OUTPUTS

◆ Roles

◆ Competencies: The Heart of the Study

◆ Competency Groupings

◆ Outputs

◆ Section Summary

SECTION 5 RESULTS OF THE STUDY

SECTION 6 ETHICAL CHALLENGES

SECTION 7 SUGGESTED AUDIENCES AND USES

SECTION 8 CONCLUSION

This section summarizes WLP roles, competencies, and outputs. It begins by describing the WLP roles, tracing their evolution from earlier ASTD studies, and emphasizing their importance. It then reviews WLP competencies and concludes with a description of outputs.

Roles

Roles represent a grouping of competencies targeted to meet specific expectations of a job or function. These roles are *not* synonymous with job titles. A WLP practitioner may perform several, if not all, of the different roles. Some WLP practitioners will only perform certain roles in the context of their jobs. Most likely, however, WLP practitioners will perform several roles at the same time.

WLP Roles

ASTD has identified seven WLP roles:

1. A *manager* plans, organizes, schedules, monitors, and leads the work of individuals and groups to attain desired results; facilitates the strategic plan; ensures that WLP is aligned with organizational needs and plans; and ensures accomplishment of the administrative requirements of the function.
2. An *analyst* troubleshoots and isolates the causes of human performance gaps or identifies areas for improving human performance.
3. An *intervention selector* chooses appropriate interventions to address root causes of human performance gaps.
4. An *intervention designer and developer* creates learning and other interventions that help to address the specific root causes of human performance gaps. Some examples of the work of the intervention designer and developer include serving as instructional designer, media specialist, materials developer, process engineer, ergonomics engineer, instructional writer, and compensation analyst.
5. An *intervention implementor* ensures the appropriate and effective implementation of desired interventions that address the specific root causes of human performance gaps. Some examples of the work of the intervention implementor include serving as administrator, instructor, organization development practitioner, career development specialist, process re-design consultant, workspace designer, compensation specialist, and facilitator.
6. A *change leader* inspires the workforce to embrace the change, creates a direction for the change effort, helps the organization's workforce to adapt to the change, and ensures that interventions are continu-

ously monitored and guided in ways consistent with stakeholders' desired results.
7. An *evaluator* assesses the impact of interventions and provides participants and stakeholders with information about the effectiveness of the intervention implementation.

These roles represent the evolution of the roles identified in previous ASTD competency studies. They accommodate the needs of those WLP practitioners who specialize in one intervention area (for example, training), as well as the needs of those who work in situations where WLP is expanding into an organizational consulting function that specifically addresses the area of HPI. The WLP roles represent a revisitation and refinement of the roles McLagan (1989) presented in *Models for HRD Practice*. They also represent a reemphasis and expansion of the roles of HPI. The need for this expansion is the direct result of looking at the new responsibilities that WLP practitioners probably will perform over the next five years. Figure 4.1 shows the relationship between the WLP roles and the HPI process model.

◆ ◆ ◆

Roles represent a grouping of competencies targeted to meet specific expectations of a job or function.

◆ ◆ ◆

The Evolution of Roles

The roles of the specialist in the WLP field have changed over the years, as has the primary focus of the competency studies. *A Study of Professional Training and Development Roles and Competencies* (Pinto & Walker, 1978) focused only on training and discussed work activities more than roles. With the publication of *Models for Excellence* (McLagan & McCullough, 1983), roles became key to grouping competencies and outputs and making sense of their meanings. The roles described in the 1983 study were appropriate for training and development only and were not appropriate for the broader roles of HRD, which were subsequently described in *Models for HRD Practice* (McLagan, 1989). That study set the pattern for future studies by focusing on current competencies, roles, and outputs of the HRD profession.

Interestingly, although the field has grown more complex, the number of identified roles has decreased. Between the 1983 and 1989 studies, the number of

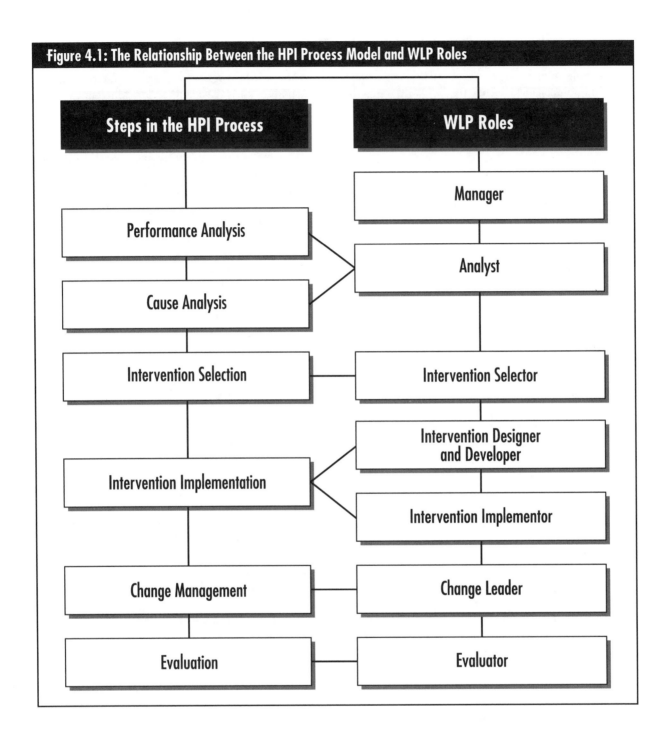

Figure 4.1: The Relationship Between the HPI Process Model and WLP Roles

Steps in the HPI Process	WLP Roles
	Manager
Performance Analysis	Analyst
Cause Analysis	
Intervention Selection	Intervention Selector
Intervention Implementation	Intervention Designer and Developer
	Intervention Implementor
Change Management	Change Leader
Evaluation	Evaluator

roles declined from 15 to 11, but the field broadened from training and development to HRD, which encompassed organization development, career development, and training and development. Likewise, the HPI roles described in *ASTD Models for Human Performance Improvement* (Rothwell, 1996a), represented a further expansion of the field, yet comprised only four roles. Table 4.1 illustrates the roles described in previous ASTD studies and shows how they relate to each other. The roles established in *ASTD Models for Learning Technologies* (Piskurich & Sanders, 1998) are intentionally not included in this list, because that study did not examine an entire field of practice. Instead, it focused on the specific issues involved in implementing learning technologies within an organization. By their very definition—electronic technologies that deliver informa-

tion and facilitate the development of skills and knowledge—learning technologies are a subset of the training and development discipline. Therefore, they are not parallel to training, HRD, HPI, or WLP competencies.

The Importance of Changing Roles in the Field
Changing roles in the field are important as indicators of changing expectations. Few observers of the WLP field can dispute that expectations for practitioners in that field have been changing. Today's WLP practitioners must meet lofty, and sometimes conflicting, expectations.

One expectation is that those practitioners today must be champions of learning in their organizations, and, at the same time, they must demonstrate sensitivity to bottom-line results, such as return-on-investment

Table 4.1: Comparisons of Roles by Competency Study

Models for Excellence	Models for HRD Practice	The ASTD Models for Human Performance Improvement	The ASTD Models for Workplace Learning and Performance
Manager of Training and Development: The role of planning, organizing, staffing, and controlling training and development operations or training and development projects and of linking training and development operations to the operations of other organization units.	**HRD Manager:** The role of supporting and leading a group's work and linking that work to the total organization.		**Manager:** The role of planning, organizing, scheduling, and leading the work of individuals and groups to attain desired results; facilitating the strategic plan; ensuring that WLP is aligned with organizational needs and plans; and ensuring the accomplishment of the administrative requirements of the function.
Strategist: The role of developing long-range plans for the training and development structure, organization, direction, policies, programs, services, and practices in order to accomplish the training and development mission.			**Manager:** The role of planning, organizing, scheduling, and leading the work of individuals and groups to attain desired results; facilitating the strategic plan; ensuring that WLP is aligned with organizational needs and plans; and ensuring the accomplishment of the administrative requirements of the function.

Models for Excellence	Models for HRD Practice	The ASTD Models for Human Performance Improvement	The ASTD Models for Workplace Learning and Performance
Theoretician: The role of developing and testing theories of learning, training, and development.	**Researcher:** The role of identifying, developing, or testing new information (theory, research, concepts, technology, models, hardware) and translating the information into implications for improved individual or organizational performance.		**Manager:** The role of planning, organizing, scheduling, and leading the work of individuals and groups to attain desired results; facilitating the strategic plan; ensuring that WLP is aligned with organizational needs and plans; and ensuring the accomplishment of the administrative requirements of the function.
Program Administrator: The role of ensuring that the facilities, equipment, materials, participants, and other components of a learning event are present and that program logistics run smoothly.	**Administrator:** The role of providing coordination and support services for the delivery of HRD programs and services.		**Intervention Implementor:** The role of ensuring the appropriate and effective implementation of desired interventions to address the specific root causes of human performance gaps. Some examples of the work of the intervention implementor include serving as administrator, instructor, organization development practitioner, career development specialist, process redesign consultant, workspace designer, compensation specialist, and facilitator.
Needs Analyst: The role of defining gaps between ideal and actual performance and specifying the cause of the gaps.	**Needs Analyst:** The role of identifying ideal and actual performance and performance conditions and determining the causes of discrepancies between them.	**Analyst:** The role of "troubleshooting to isolate the cause(s) of human performance gaps or identifying areas in which human performance can be improved."	**Analyst:** The role of "troubleshooting to isolate the cause(s) of human performance gaps or identifying areas in which human performance can be improved."
Task analyst: The role of identifying activities, tasks, subtasks, and human resource and support requirements necessary to accomplish specific results in a job or organization.			**Analyst:** The role of "troubleshooting to isolate the cause(s) of human performance gaps or identifying areas in which human performance can be improved."

Models for Excellence	Models for HRD Practice	The ASTD Models for Human Performance Improvement	The ASTD Models for Workplace Learning and Performance
Individual Development Counselor: The role of helping an individual to assess personal competencies, values, and goals and to identify and plan development and career actions.	**Individual Career Development advisor:** The role of helping individuals to assess personal competencies, values, and goals and to identify, plan, and implement development and career actions.		**Intervention Implementor:** The role of ensuring the appropriate and effective implementation of desired interventions to address the specific root cause(s) of human performance gaps. Some examples of the work of the intervention implementor include serving as administrator, instructor, organization development practitioner, career development specialist, process redesign consultant, workspace designer, compensation specialist, and facilitator.
Program Designer: The role of preparing objectives, defining content, and selecting and sequencing activities for a specific program.	**Program Designer:** The role of preparing objectives, defining content, and selecting and sequencing activities for a specific intervention.	**Intervention Specialist:** The role of selecting "appropriate interventions to address the root cause(s) of performance gaps."	**Intervention Designer and Developer:** The role of creating learning and other interventions that help to address the specific root causes of human performance gaps. Some examples of the work of the intervention designer and developer include serving as instructional designer, media specialist, materials developer, process engineer, ergonomics engineer, instructional writer, and compensation analyst.

Models for Excellence	Models for HRD Practice	The ASTD Models for Human Performance Improvement	The ASTD Models for Workplace Learning and Performance
Media Specialist: The role of producing software and using audio, visual, computer, and other hardware-based technologies for training and development.	**HRD Materials Developer:** The role of producing written or electronically mediated instructional materials.		**Intervention Designer and Developer:** The role of creating learning and other interventions that help to address the specific root causes of human performance gaps. Some examples of the work of the intervention designer and developer include serving as instructional designer, media specialist, materials developer, process engineer, ergonomics engineer, instructional writer, and compensation analyst.
Instructional Writer: The role of preparing written learning and instructional materials.	**HRD Materials Developer:** The role of producing written or electronically mediated instructional materials.		**Intervention Designer and Developer:** The role of creating learning and other interventions that help to address the specific root causes of human performance gaps. Some examples of the work of the intervention designer and developer include serving as instructional designer, media specialist, materials developer, process engineer, ergonomics engineer, instructional writer, and compensation analyst.
Marketer: The role of selling training and development viewpoints, learning packages, programs, and services to target audiences outside one's own work unit.	**Marketer:** The role of marketing and contracting for HRD viewpoints, programs, and services.		**Change Leader:** The role of inspiring the workforce to embrace the change, creating a direction for the change effort, helping the organization's workforce to adapt to the change, and ensuring that interventions are continuously monitored and guided in ways consistent with stakeholders' desired results.

Models for Excellence	Models for HRD Practice	The ASTD Models for Human Performance Improvement	The ASTD Models for Workplace Learning and Performance
Instructor: The role of presenting information and directing structured learning experiences so that individuals learn.	**Instructor/Facilitator:** The role of presenting information, directing structured learning experiences, and managing group discussion and group processes.		**Intervention Implementor:** The role of ensuring that desired interventions are appropriately and effectively implemented to address the specific root causes of human performance gaps. Some examples of the work of the intervention implementor include serving as administrator, instructor, organization development practitioner, career development specialist, process redesign consultant, workspace designer, compensation specialist, and facilitator.
Group Facilitator: The role of managing group discussions and group processes so that individuals learn and group members feel the experience is positive.	**Instructor/Facilitator:** The role of presenting information, directing structured learning experiences, and managing group discussion and group processes.		**Intervention Implementor:** The role of ensuring that desired interventions are appropriately and effectively implemented to address the specific root causes of human performance gaps. Some examples of the work of the intervention implementor include serving as administrator, instructor, organization development practitioner, career development specialist, process redesign consultant, workspace designer, compensation specialist, and facilitator.

Models for Excellence	Models for HRD Practice	The ASTD Models for Human Performance Improvement	The ASTD Models for Workplace Learning and Performance
Evaluator: The role of identifying the impact of a program, service, or product.	**Evaluator:** The role of identifying the impact of an intervention on individual or organizational effectiveness.	**Evaluator:** The role of assessing the impact of interventions and following up on changes made, actions taken, and results achieved in order to provide participants and stakeholders with information about how well interventions are being implemented.	**Evaluator:** The role of assessing the impact of interventions and following up on changes made, actions taken, and results achieved in order to provide participants and stakeholders with information about how well interventions are being implemented.
Transfer Agent: The role of helping individuals apply learning after the learning experience.	**Organization Change Agent:** The role of influencing and supporting changes in organization behavior.	**Change Manager:** The role of ensuring the implementation of interventions in ways consistent with desired results and ensuring that they help individuals and groups achieve results.	**Change leader:** The role of inspiring the workforce to embrace the change, creating a direction for the change effort, helping the organization's workforce to adapt to the change, and ensuring that interventions are continuously monitored and guided in ways consistent with stakeholders' desired results.

and improved performance. Many contemporary organizations consider the offering of training programs only as inadequate. Today's WLP practitioners must be prepared to offer any intervention that will improve productivity.

Another recent expectation is that practitioners must be the masters of practical, workplace-based learning interventions. They can no longer afford to think in terms of single-medium delivery, such as classroom instruction. They must, instead, be increasingly conversant with a range of delivery methods—from high-tech offerings (such as Web-based or satellite TV instruction) to time-honored low-tech offerings (such as improved one-on-one coaching or on-the-job training). Furthermore, WLP practitioners must be able to combine delivery media and conduct cost comparisons to match the best technologies with identified learning needs.

A third expectation is that those who work in WLP be familiar with a range of change strategies. These strategies include everything—intrapersonal interventions (for example, building new competencies for a single employee), intragroup interventions (for example,

solving a group's conflicts), and intergroup interventions (for example, improving the communication process among two or more groups), for example.

By understanding these evolving expectations, individuals who perform WLP work can gain a keener perspective on how best to meet them. The WLP roles provide an effective and user-friendly method for understanding and acquiring the competencies needed to meet these new expectations.

The Implications of the WLP Roles

The new roles listed for WLP match the new expectations affecting those who perform WLP work. Organizations expect WLP practitioners to do more than merely conduct training needs assessments, design and deliver training, or evaluate how much people liked or can apply the training they received. The future will demand a more holistic understanding of the many variables that affect performance and learning in the workplace. Organizations will expect WLP practitioners to do the following:

- Analyze performance problems and learning needs, and select learning or other interventions that solve productivity problems or build intellectual capital.
- Select appropriate strategies that meet identified needs.
- Design and develop (or coordinate with external intervention specialists who can design and develop) appropriate interventions to meet identified needs. One WLP practitioner is not likely to possess all of the skills necessary to implement the broad array of interventions necessary to solve all types of performance problems. For instance, most professional WLP practitioners are not likely to have extensive experience with workspace or ergonomic design. In these cases, the professional WLP practitioner would hire and coordinate with a specialist in the needed field.)
- Implement the results successfully by monitoring the implementation schedule and helping individuals understand the vital role they play in the overall strategy.
- Assure that all activities associated with the intervention plan are aligned with organizational goals and needs.
- Continuously evaluate results at the individual, group, and organizational levels.

The seven WLP roles align WLP competencies with these expectations. Similarly, the WLP roles represent an evolutionary melding and alignment of the roles presented in *Models for HRD Practice* (McLagan, 1989) with the roles presented in *ASTD Models for Human Performance Improvement* (Rothwell, 1996a). Although not identical to the roles in either of these previous studies, the WLP roles are not inconsistent with those in the previous studies.

Competencies: The Heart of the Study

Previous ASTD competency studies made significant contributions by defining the field and the nature of the work conducted by professional practitioners. To accomplish this goal, studies like *Models for Excellence* (McLagan & McCullough, 1983), *Models for HRD Practice* and *ASTD Models for Human Performance Improvement* determined the outputs generated by practitioners, grouped the outputs into roles, and then derived the competencies necessary to successfully perform the roles and produce the identified outputs. This methodology is logical and appropriate for determining and defining what exists.

The primary purpose of the study was to define not only the current state of the field but also a vision of the field in the next five years. In a departure from previous competency studies, this study began with competencies, grouped the competencies into seven roles, and provided sample outputs for each role. An underlying assumption of this approach is that it is possible to identify key competencies needed for the future success of the WLP practitioner in the field. The difficulty came in accurately determining the outputs that organizations will expect in the future. The role of technology, and specifically the Internet, exemplifies this point. Clearly the Internet and technology will have a tremendous impact on the WLP field over the next five years. Although predicting exactly what changes technology will bring to WLP is nearly impossible, the competencies associated with implementing technologies within an organization will remain important and relatively consistent.

Competency Groupings

The competencies for WLP fall into six categories or groupings: analytical, business, interpersonal, leadership, technical, and technological. Following are descriptions of each competency grouping as well as a list of the associated competencies. (Table 4.2 provides descriptions of the competencies. Table 4.3 lists the roles associated with each competency.)

Analytical competencies are associated with the creation of new understandings or methods through the synthesis of multiple ideas, processes, and data. The following competencies compose this group:

- analytical thinking
- analyzing performance data
- career development theory and application
- competency identification
- intervention selection
- knowledge management
- model building
- organization development theory and application
- performance gap analysis
- performance theory
- process consultation
- reward system theory and application
- social awareness
- staff selection theory and application
- standards identification
- systems thinking
- training theory and application
- work environment analysis
- workplace performance, learning strategies, and intervention evaluation.

Business competencies are associated with the understanding of organizations as systems, and of the processes, decision criteria, issues, and implications of the operational units of the non-WLP aspects of the organization (for example, production, operations, finance, customer service, sales, administrative services). The following competencies compose this group:

- ability to see the "big picture"
- business knowledge
- cost/benefit analysis
- evaluation of results against organizational goals
- identification of critical business issues
- industry awareness
- knowledge capital
- negotiating/contracting
- outsourcing management
- project management
- quality implications.

Interpersonal competencies are associated with the understanding and application of methods that produce effective interactions of people and groups. The following competencies compose this group:

- communication
- communication networks
- consulting
- coping skills
- interpersonal relationship building.

Leadership competencies are associated with influencing, enabling, or inspiring others to act. The following competencies compose this group:

- buy-in/advocacy
- diversity awareness
- ethics modeling
- goal implementation
- group dynamics
- leadership
- visioning.

Technical competencies are associated with the understanding and application of existing knowledge or processes. The following competencies compose this group:

- adult learning
- facilitation
- feedback
- intervention monitoring
- questioning
- survey design and development.

Technological competencies are those competencies associated with the understanding and appropriate application of current or emerging technology. The following competencies compose this group:

- computer-mediated communication
- distance education
- electronic performance support systems
- technological literacy.

Outputs

Models for HRD Practice (McLagan, 1989) defines an *output* as "a product or service that an individual or group delivers to others, especially to colleagues, customers, or clients" (p. 77). According to one of several mainstream competency identification and assessment methodologies, outputs are an important starting point

Table 4.2: Competencies for WLP

Analytical Competencies	Description
Analytical Thinking	Clarifying complex issues by breaking them down into meaningful components and synthesizing related items
Analyzing Performance Data	Interpreting performance data and determining the effect of interventions on customers, suppliers, and employees
Career Development Theory and Application	Understanding the theories, techniques, and appropriate applications of career development interventions used for performance improvement
Competency Identification	Identifying the skills, knowledge, and attitudes required to perform work
Intervention Selection	Selecting performance improvement strategies that address the root cause(s) of performance gaps rather than treat symptoms or side effects
Knowledge Management	Developing and implementing systems for creating, managing, and distributing knowledge
Model Building	Conceptualizing and developing theoretical and practical frameworks that describe complex ideas
Organization Development Theory and Application	Understanding the theories, techniques, and appropriate applications of organization development interventions as they are used for performance improvement
Performance Gap Analysis	Performing "front-end analysis" by comparing actual and ideal performance levels in the workplace; identifying opportunities and strategies for performance improvement
Performance Theory	Recognizing the implications, outcomes, and consequences of performance interventions to distinguish between activities and results
Process Consultation	Using a monitoring and feedback method to continually improve the productivity of work groups
Reward System Theory and Application	Understanding the theories, techniques, and appropriate applications of reward system interventions used for performance improvement
Social Awareness	Seeing organizations as dynamic political, economic, and social systems
Staff Selection Theory and Application	Understanding the theories, techniques, and appropriate applications of staff selection interventions used for performance improvement
Standards Identification	Determining what constitutes success for individuals, organizations, and processes
Systems Thinking	Recognizing the interrelationships among events by determining the driving forces that connect seemingly isolated incidents within the organization; taking a holistic view of performance problems in order to find root causes

Table 4.2: Competencies for WLP (continued)

Analytical Competencies	Description
Training Theory and Application	Understanding the theories, techniques, and appropriate applications of training interventions used for performance improvement
Work Environment Analysis	Examining the work environment for issues or characteristics that affect human performance; understanding characteristics of a high-performance workplace
Workplace Performance, Learning Strategies, and Intervention Evaluation	Continually evaluating and improving interventions before and during implementation

Business Competencies	Description
Ability to See the "Big Picture"	Identifying trends and patterns that are outside the normal paradigm of the organization
Business Knowledge	Demonstrating awareness of business functions and how business decisions affect financial and nonfinancial work results
Cost/Benefit Analysis	Accurately assessing the relative value of performance improvement interventions
Evaluation of Results Against Organizational Goals	Assessing how well workplace performance, learning strategies, and results match organizational goals and strategic intent
Identification of Critical Business Issues	Determining key business issues and forces for change and applying that knowledge to performance improvement strategies
Industry Awareness	Understanding the current and future climate of the organization's industry and formulating strategies that respond to that climate
Knowledge Capital	Measuring knowledge capital and determining its value to the organization
Negotiating/Contracting	Organizing, preparing, monitoring, and evaluating work performed by vendors and consultants
Outsourcing Management	Ability to identify and select specialized resources outside of the organization; identifying, selecting, and managing technical specifications for these specialized resources
Project Management	Planning, organizing, and monitoring work
Quality Implications	Identifying the relationships and implications among quality programs and performance

Interpersonal Competencies	Description
Communication	Applying effective verbal, nonverbal, and written communication methods to achieve desired results

Communication Networks	Understanding the various methods through which communication is achieved
Consulting	Understanding the results that stakeholders desire from a process and providing insight into how they can best use their resources to achieve goals
Coping Skills	Dealing with ambiguity and stress resulting from conflicting information and goals; helping others deal with ambiguity and stress
Interpersonal Relationship Building	Effectively interacting with others in order to produce meaningful outcomes

Leadership Competencies	Description
Buy-in/Advocacy	Building ownership and support for workplace initiatives
Diversity Awareness	Assessing the impact and appropriateness of interventions on individuals, groups, and organizations
Ethics Modeling	Modeling exemplary ethical behavior and understanding the implications of this responsibility
Goal Implementation	Ensuring that goals are converted into efficient actions; getting results despite conflicting priorities, lack of resources, or ambiguity
Group Dynamics	Assessing how groups of people function and evolve as they seek to meet the needs of their members and of the organization
Leadership	Leading, influencing, and coaching others to help them achieve desired results
Visioning	Seeing the possibilities of "what can be" and inspiring a shared sense of purpose within the organization

Technical Competencies	Description
Adult Learning	Understanding how adults learn and how they use knowledge, skills, and attitudes
Facilitation	Helping others to discover new insights
Feedback	Providing performance information to the appropriate people
Intervention Monitoring	Tracking and coordinating interventions to assure consistency in implementation and alignment with organizational strategies
Questioning	Collecting data via pertinent questions asked during surveys, interviews, and focus groups for the purpose of performance analysis

Table 4.2: Competencies for WLP (continued)

Technical Competencies (continued)	Description
Survey Design and Development	Creating survey approaches that use open-ended (essay) and closed-style questions (multiple choice and Likert items) for collecting data; preparing instruments in written, verbal, or electronic formats

Technological Competencies	Description
Computer-Mediated Communication	Understanding the implication of current and evolving computer-based electronic communication
Distance Education	Understanding the evolving trends in technology-supported delivery methods and the implications of separating instructors and learners in time and location
Electronic Performance Support Systems	Understanding current and evolving performance support systems and their appropriate applications
Technological Literacy	Understanding and appropriately applying existing, new, or emerging technology

Table 4.3: WLP Roles and Associated Competencies

Competencies	Manager	Analyst	Selector[1]	Designer[2]	Implementor[3]	Change Leader[4]	Evaluator
Analytical Competencies							
Analytical Thinking	✕	✕				✕	✕
Analyzing Performance Data			✕	✕		✕	✕
Career Development Theory and Application	✕		✕	✕		✕	
Competency Identification	✕	✕					
Intervention Selection			✕	✕			
Knowledge Management	✕		✕	✕		✕	
Model Building		✕		✕		✕	
Organization Development Theory and Application	✕		✕	✕		✕	
Performance Gap Analysis	✕	✕	✕				✕
Performance Theory	✕	✕	✕	✕		✕	✕
Process Consultation	✕				✕	✕	
Reward System Theory and Application	✕		✕	✕		✕	
Social Awareness	✕	✕				✕	
Staff Selection Theory and Application	✕		✕			✕	
Standards Identification	✕	✕		✕		✕	✕
Systems Thinking	✕	✕	✕	✕		✕	✕
Training Theory and Application			✕	✕	✕	✕	
Work Environment Analysis	✕	✕				✕	✕
Workplace Performance, Learning Strategies, and Intervention Evaluation				✕	✕	✕	✕

[1] Intervention selector.
[2] Intervention designer and developer.
[3] Intervention implementor.
[4] Change leader.

Competencies	Roles						
	Manager	Analyst	Selector[1]	Designer[2]	Implementor[3]	Change Leader[4]	Evaluator
Business Competencies							
Ability to See the "Big Picture"	×	×				×	×
Business Knowledge	×	×				×	
Cost/Benefit Analysis	×		×				×
Evaluation of Results Against Organizational Goals	×					×	×
Identification of Critical Business Issues	×	×	×			×	
Industry Awareness	×	×	×	×		×	
Knowledge Capital	×					×	×
Negotiating/Contracting	×						
Outsourcing Management	×		×			×	
Project Management	×			×		×	
Quality Implications	×	×	×			×	×
Interpersonal Competencies							
Communication	×	×	×	×	×	×	×
Communication Networks	×	×	×	×	×	×	×
Consulting	×		×		×	×	
Coping Skills	×	×			×	×	
Interpersonal Relationship Building	×	×	×	×	×	×	×

[1] Intervention selector.

[2] Intervention designer and developer.

[3] Intervention implementor.

[4] Change leader.

Competencies	Roles						
	Manager	Analyst	S[1] Selector	D[2] Designer	I[3] Implementor	C[4] Change Leader	Evaluator
Leadership Competencies							
Buy-in/Advocacy	×		×		×	×	
Diversity Awareness	×		×	×	×	×	
Ethics Modeling	×	×	×	×		×	
Group Dynamics	×	×			×	×	
Leadership	×					×	
Visioning	×					×	
Technical Competencies							
Adult Learning			×	×	×	×	
Facilitation	×				×	×	
Feedback	×					×	×
Intervention Monitoring					×	×	×
Questioning		×					×
Survey Design and Development		×		×			
Technological Competencies							
Computer-Mediated Communication	×		×	×	×	×	
Distance Education			×	×			
Electronic Performance Support Systems			×	×	×		
Technological Literacy	×	×	×	×	×	×	×

[1] Intervention selector.
[2] Intervention designer and developer.
[3] Intervention implementor.
[4] Change leader.

for determining what competencies are necessary for exemplary work performance in a job, team, division, department, function, or organization. That logic is seemingly irrefutable: start with desired results and work backwards.

Due to rapidly changing environmental conditions, however, expectations for performers do not remain static. In fact, expectations for successful performance are changing faster than ever before. Although one can determine outputs for *present* success with some certainty, one rarely can determine outputs for *future* success with any degree of accuracy. For example, today's software engineers cannot predict with certainty what the output of the next generation of software will be. They may know, for instance, that one output of a word-processing program will be a printed page, but they may not know whether to create other outputs for use on the Web, with voice, or with desktop videophones. A future-oriented competency study, then, must reconsider the nature of outputs. Competencies do not change at the same rapid rate as outputs do. Competency descriptions are general in nature and applicable to a broad array of outputs. For instance, technological literacy will always be a valid competency description regardless of how much technology changes in the future. What will change are the specific skills and knowledge that constitute technological literacy. Currently a working knowledge of personal computers, network computing, word processing, browser technology, and various software applications constitute technological competency. In five years, however, users will need a more intimate knowledge of database applications, Web-based teleconferencing technology, and various collaborative software applications.

Another problem with outputs is that they make it appear that all outputs for the field are similar across all corporate cultures. That one-size-fits-all logic is not realistic, as most WLP practitioners know all too well. Different stakeholders—the customers of WLP efforts—value different outputs with varying weights and also assign different quality requirements to them.

Outputs by WLP Role

The term *sample output* describes the general expectations for achieving results. Stated in another way, a sample output is an approximation of desired results intended for guidance, rather than the precise results required themselves. It is an applied form of the fuzzy logic (approximations) used in artificial intelligence.

For purposes of this study, table 4.4 depicts sample outputs by WLP role. These are dynamic outputs because they are constantly changing to meet the current environment. Every output must align with its intended objective. If the stated output does not help one

to reach a stated objective, then one must seek more appropriate outputs. For instance, in a business environment, all outputs must have some type of financial gain. That is, they must help the company to improve its bottom line. Therefore, a list of business-related outputs must include items such as "links intervention design to business objectives" and "contributes to substantial returns-on-investment for all shareholders." In a government institution, all outputs must support the organization's objectives for serving the taxpayers, which may include outputs such as "delivering quality services in a cost-effective manner." As section seven notes, this book is intended for people in all types of organizations. Therefore, many of the sample outputs are generic enough to apply to a variety of organizational settings (that is, corporate, government, nonprofit, academic). In practice, however, the user must customize all of these outputs to fit the organizational setting.

A Process for Determining Culturally Specific Outputs

The process of discovering the outputs desired at any time is akin to the process of discovering the new products or services desired by customers or clients. The needs and expectations of the unique organizational culture should be a priority. A process for establishing and using WLP outputs must include the following steps:

1. List the competencies from this study that are appropriate to the unique work and organizational culture being considered. If possible, have stakeholders determine what competencies WLP practitioners should demonstrate in the future.
2. Determine the types of information that stakeholders feel will help the organization to meet its needs. Identify specific shortcomings of previous outputs as a basis for this step.
3. Brainstorm a list of outputs that would appropriately demonstrate each competency within your culture. (For example, survey design and development outputs might include a valid and reliable survey questionnaire on paper or on the Web.)
4. Have stakeholders (or others who are very familiar with the organization) review and make recommendations on the list of outputs. Make sure that these outputs align with the organization's objectives and in corporate settings, with the financial goals.
5. Add quality requirements to the outputs by posing the following questions:

   ◆ What are the minimum requirements for each output? Consider elements of quality, quantity, cost, time, and customer service.

Table 4.4: Sample Outputs of WLP Work by Role

Role	Sample Outputs
Manager: Plans, organizes, schedules, and leads the work of individuals and groups to attain desired results; facilitates the strategic plan; ensures that WLP is aligned with organizational needs and plans; and ensures the accomplishment of the administrative requirements of the function	<ul><li>WLP plans for the organization or unit</li><li>Strategies that align WLP efforts with organizational and individual needs</li><li>Work plans for WLP efforts</li><li>Plans to secure the human talent to carry out WLP efforts</li><li>Objectives that support desired business results</li></ul>
Analyst: Isolates and toubleshoots the causes of human performance gaps or identifies areas for the improvement of human performance	<ul><li>Analytical methods that uncover the root causes of performance gaps</li><li>Results of assessment</li><li>Reports to key stakeholders of individual, group, or organizational change efforts about directions of such efforts</li><li>Reports to executives that highlight the relationship between human performance and financial performance</li></ul>
Intervention Selector: Selects appropriate WLP and non-WLP interventions to address root causes of human performance gaps	<ul><li>Recommendations to others about selecting interventions to address or avert problems or seize opportunities</li><li>Recommendations to others about ways to combine interventions</li><li>Assessments of the expected impact of interventions</li><li>Objectives for interventions that are aligned with desired business results</li></ul>
Intervention Designer and Developer: Designs and develops interventions that help to address the specific root causes of human performance gaps and that effectively compliment other WLP or non-WLP interventions targeted at achieving similar results	<ul><li>Intervention designs</li><li>Action plans for interventions</li><li>Lists of stakeholders and participants for interventions</li><li>Links intervention design to business objectives</li></ul>
Intervention Implementor: Ensures the appropriate and effective implementation of desired interventions to address the specific root causes of human performance gaps in a manner that effectively compliment other WLP or non-WLP interventions targeted at achieving similar results	<ul><li>Plans and schedules for implementing interventions</li><li>Facilitation methods that will deliver the intervention appropriately</li><li>Consulting services</li><li>Contributions to business goals and objectives</li><li>Measurable return-on-investment</li></ul>
Change Leader: Inspires the workforce to embrace the change, creates a direction for the change effort, helps the organization's workforce to adapt to the change, and ensures that interventions are continuously monitored and guided in ways consistent with stakeholders' desired results.	<ul><li>Revised implementation plans that reflect changes in the original intervention strategy</li><li>Periodic reports to key stakeholders of interventions about their progress</li><li>Written illustrations of successful implementation cases</li></ul>
Evaluator: Assesses the impact of interventions and follows up on changes made, actions taken, and results achieved in order to provide participants and stakeholders with information about the effectiveness of intervention implementation.	<ul><li>Reports that show the evaluation results</li><li>Recommendations for future WLP interventions</li><li>Reports that determine if intervention results caused a positive impact on business objectives</li></ul>

- What are the desired requirements for each output?
- How may requirements change over time?
- What distinguishes exemplary outputs from average outputs?

Figure 4.2 depicts these outputs. Use the worksheet appearing in figure 4.3 to structure your thinking about the most critical outputs in your unique corporate culture.

Section Summary

Section four described WLP roles, competencies, and outputs. It has provided a list of what those roles are, explained why they are important, and traced their evolution from earlier studies. The section also identified the competencies and outputs for WLP.

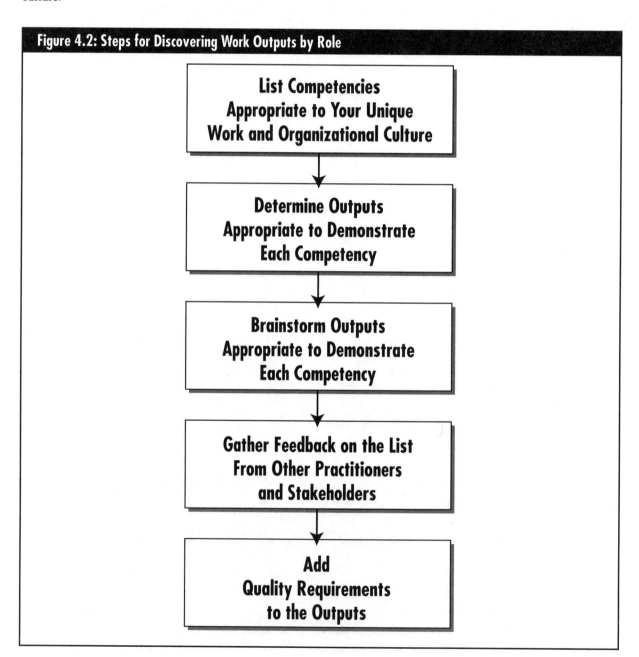

Figure 4.2: Steps for Discovering Work Outputs by Role

List Competencies Appropriate to Your Unique Work and Organizational Culture

Determine Outputs Appropriate to Demonstrate Each Competency

Brainstorm Outputs Appropriate to Demonstrate Each Competency

Gather Feedback on the List From Other Practitioners and Stakeholders

Add Quality Requirements to the Outputs

Figure 4.3: A Worksheet for Discovering Outputs

Directions: Use this worksheet to help you discover the outputs expected of you in your WLP work in your corporate culture. First, examine the competencies described in this book. Select those appropriate to your organization and your position and insert them in the left column below. Add paper as necessary. Then, for each competency, brainstorm a list of outputs expected for each competency that you, other WLP practitioners, and stakeholders inside and outside your organization expect for that competency and that are linked to present or future work success. Although no answers are right or wrong in any absolute sense, some may be right or wrong for your organization at a given time.

Competencies	Outputs

The preceding chapters supplied comprehensive lists of the competencies, roles, and outputs necessary for WLP work. Although the main purpose of the study was to generate and validate these lists, the study results also provide great insight into the different perspectives of the three primary respondent groups (that is, WLP experts, WLP practitioners, and line managers who use WLP services). By examining the differences and similarities of these perspectives, one can develop a clearer picture of the future. This section will address the following types of questions:

◆ How different or similar were the perspectives of the three respondent groups?
◆ What types of skills do line managers expect WLP professionals to have in the near future?
◆ How well equipped are people in the WLP profession for meeting these expectations?
◆ What types of competencies (that is, analytical, technical, leadership, technological, business, or interpersonal) should a WLP professional begin developing immediately?

Answering all of these questions requires first a summary look at the data for each group and then a synthesis of the data into some meaningful messages.

Recall from section three that the questionnaire asked respondents to rate each competency on a scale of 1 to 5, with 5 indicating a high degree of importance. Respondents rated current and future competencies on this scale. Note that this section does not rely on measures of statistical significance to make its points. Instead, a simple measure of .50 (that is, a 10 percent difference on the scale of 1 to 5) or greater between current and future means indicates that a group's response anticipates a meaningful change in the next five years. Some of these increases may have occurred due to random chance, but it's unlikely. Although a true statistician might find such an approach difficult to digest, the presentation of the results will be accessible and meaningful to the readers of this book.

This approach will help readers to avoid getting caught up in numbers and statistics and instead will help them to spot the patterns that reside within the data. The size of the respondent subgroups is not large enough to allow statistical inferences. This study does not intend to prove beyond a reasonable doubt that the competencies listed are the only ones necessary for WLP work. Instead, this study provides clear evidence of what the respondents consider to be the essentials of WLP work, and it recommends ways of building on this new knowledge. This volume is a guidebook, not a rule book. The true strength of this study lies in the re-

search design, which used three distinct respondent groups to validate the information provided.

Of particular interest is the tendency of certain groups to select particular competency groupings, and this section compares those groupings. For now, note that tables 5.1, 5.3, and 5.5 provide the competency grouping associated with each competency. The grouping is in the same cell as the competency name and is noted in brackets (for example, [Analytical]). See figure 4.3 in the preceding section for a complete list of the competencies within each grouping. Recall from that section the following competency groupings:

◆ *Analytical:* Competencies that create new understandings or methods through a synthesis of multiple ideas, processes, and data.
◆ *Business:* Competencies associated with the understanding of organizations as systems and of the processes, decision criteria, issues, and implications of the non-WLP aspects of the organization.
◆ *Interpersonal:* Competencies associated with the understanding and application of methods that produce effective interactions of people and groups.
◆ *Leadership:* Competencies associated with influencing, enabling, or inspiring others to act.
◆ *Technical:* Competencies associated with the understanding and application of existing knowledge or processes.
◆ *Technological:* Competencies associated with the understanding and appropriate application of current or emerging technology.

The total number of possible competencies under each competency grouping are

◆ analytical competencies—19
◆ business competencies—11
◆ interpersonal competencies—5
◆ leadership competencies—7
◆ technical competencies—6
◆ technological competencies—4.

The tables in this section provide the mean (average) current and future scores for each group and the difference between the current and future means. The competencies appear in descending order according to their "difference" score. Notice that all mean difference scores begin with a plus sign ("+"). This plus sign indicates that the future score was higher than the current score in all cases except where there was no difference between the scores (in only two instances were the current and future mean scores identical, once in the expert group and once in the line manager group). Had any of the competencies been identified as declining in importance in the future, a minus sign ("−") would have preceded the difference score.

Tables 5.1, 5.3, and 5.5 also provide a ranking (calculated by the mean) for each of the current and future competency scores. The competencies do not appear in rank order but according to their difference score, however, because the rankings differ between current and future time frames. The ranking number is located above the mean score in the columns marked "Current Rank (Mean)" and "Future Rank (Mean)." Note that, in many cases, two to four competencies are tied for a ranked position. For instance, in table 5.1, under the current rankings, "feedback," "intervention selection," and "industry awareness" all achieved a mean score of 3.92. This qualified each competency for seventh place in the ranking scheme. To simplify, these tables assign competencies randomly to seventh, eighth, and ninth place. Although this approach is not mathematically accurate, it makes the tables far less confusing. At the same time, reversing the order of these three competencies would not compromise the integrity of the data. In cases of ties for 10th place (the top 10 rankings appear separately), the table lists all competencies that achieved the equivalent mean. Again, the purpose of this material is to provide the reader with a feel for how the preferences and perceptions of each group stack up against each other.

These ties in rank order create another interesting phenomenon. Although most competencies saw an increase in their future scores over their current scores (all except the two competencies mentioned earlier that remained the same), some competencies appear to decline in rank order from the current list to the future list. Therefore, ranks are not useful in measuring increased or decreased importance between current and future competencies. One should not use the rankings to compare competencies across time periods (that is, across current and future lists).

To gain a better sense of the differences and similarities between the respondent groups, one must compare the difference scores of each group. This assessment is completely independent of the rankings because researchers calculated it solely from the difference between the means and did not have to take ties into consideration.

WLP Practitioner Responses
Section three provides a full accounting of the demographic makeup of the WLP practitioners who responded to the questionnaire. This practitioner group

is by far the most diverse respondent group, representing a full range of ages, races, disciplines, and experience levels. The randomness of this group provides an excellent backdrop for the consideration of the responses of the experts and line managers. On average, the WLP practitioners saw all 52 competencies increasing in importance over the next five years. Of those 52 competencies, the WLP practitioner group anticipated that 22 would increase significantly in importance (by 10 percent or more) over the next five years. In table 5.1, those competencies are listed first.

Of the 22 competencies identified as increasing in importance significantly in the future, seven are analytical competencies, seven are business competencies, four are technological competencies, two are interpersonal competencies, one is a technical competency, and one is a leadership competency. The WLP practitioners showed a very strong preference for analytical and business competencies and felt that these two areas will be essential to their career survival in the coming years. They had more diverse responses than those of the other two groups. Most WLP practitioners listed at least one competency from each competency grouping as important. They anticipated that they will need a balance of competency types for their future work in WLP, although they did emphasize analytical and business competencies.

Top-10 Competency Rankings for the WLP Practitioner Group
Another way to consider the perspective of each respondent group is to look at their top-10 choices. Remember that using rankings as a means of determining an increase or decrease in perceived importance between current and future lists is meaningless. The rankings only display the relative value of each competency either currently or in the future.

Also, do not become confused by any discussions of competency grouping related to the top-10 rankings. Remember that in table 5.1 only those competencies that achieved a difference score of +.50 or higher are specifically discussed in relation to competency groupings. Tables 5.2, 5.4, and 5.6 present the highest-rated competencies in current and future rankings, regardless of their difference scores.

Table 5.2 displays several interesting points. Four of the future competencies do not appear on the current side of the list. These four competencies are "technological literacy," "ability to see the big picture," "evaluation of results against organizational goals," and "knowledge management." All four of these competencies had difference scores that were well above the .50 level, which allowed them to leapfrog onto the future list.

Table 5.1: WLP Practitioner Responses
Competency Rankings in Order of Difference*

Competency Name [Competency Grouping]	Current Rank (Mean)	Future Rank (Mean)	Difference (Mean)
Distance Education [Technological]	48 (3.20)	24 (4.17)	(+.97)
Electronic Performance Support Systems [Technological]	50 (3.13)	33 (4.01)	(+.88)
Knowledge Management [Analytical]	30 (3.54)	11 (4.34)	(+.80)
Computer-Mediated Communication [Technological]	28 (3.57)	13 (4.32)	(+.75)
Technological Literacy [Technological]	16 (3.80)	2 (4.51)	(+.71)
Knowledge Capital [Business]	52 (2.91)	49 (3.61)	(+.70)
Outsourcing Management [Business]	49 (3.14)	45 (3.83)	(+.69)
Systems Thinking [Analytical]	39 (3.40)	28 (4.09)	(+.69)
Evaluation of Results Against Organizational Goals [Business]	21 (3.69)	10 (4.34)	(+.65)
Ability to See the "Big Picture" [Business]	18 (3.74)	9 (4.37)	(+.63)
Cost/Benefit Analysis [Business]	44 (3.32)	38 (3.95)	(+.63)
Work Environment Analysis [Analytical]	41 (3.37)	37 (3.95)	(+.58)
Analyzing Performance Data [Analytical]	25 (3.16)	23 (4.18)	(+.57)
Identification of Critical Business Issues [Business]	20 (3.70)	16 (4.27)	(+.57)
Business Knowledge [Business]	33 (3.48)	32 (4.02)	(+.54)
Reward System Theory and Application [Analytical]	45 (3.29)	46 (3.83)	(+.54)
Consulting [Interpersonal]	32 (3.51)	31 (4.04)	(+.53)

*Competencies are listed in order of their difference means. "Distance Education," the competency with the highest difference mean, appears at the top of the list; "Electronic Performance Support Systems," which has the second-highest difference mean, appears second; and so forth.

Table 5.1: WLP Practitioner Responses
Competency Rankings in Order of Difference* (continued)

Competency Name [Competency Grouping]	Current Rank (Mean)	Future Rank (Mean)	Difference (Mean)
Visioning [Leadership]	22 (3.68)	19 (4.21)	(+.53)
Career Development Theory and Application [Analytical]	43 (3.34)	42 (3.86)	(+.52)
Intervention Selection [Analytical]	7 (3.92)	5 (4.44)	(+.52)
Intervention Monitoring [Technical]	35 (3.45)	36 (3.96)	(+.51)
Communication Networks [Interpersonal]	24 (3.65)	25 (4.15)	(+.50)
Coping Skills [Interpersonal]	29 (3.55)	30 (4.04)	(+.49)
Social Awareness [Analytical]	51 (3.10)	51 (3.59)	(+.49)
Negotiating/Contracting [Business]	42 (3.35)	44 (3.83)	(+.48)
Performance Gap Analysis [Analytical]	10 (3.90)	8 (4.38)	(+.48)
Process Consultation [Analytical]	27 (3.58)	29 (4.06)	(+.48)
Industry Awareness [Business]	8 (3.92)	7 (4.38)	(+.46)
Staff Selection Theory and Application [Analytical]	37 (3.42)	41 (3.88)	(+.46)
Organization Development Theory and Application [Analytical]	40 (3.38)	43 (3.83)	(+.45)
Performance Theory [Analytical]	34 (3.47)	40 (3.92)	(+.45)
Standards Identification [Analytical]	15 (3.80)	18 (4.24)	(+.44)
Workplace Performance, Learning Strategies, and Intervention Evaluation [Analytical]	11 (3.89)	12 (4.33)	(+.44)
Buy-in/Advocacy [Leadership]	14 (3.84)	17 (4.27)	(+.43)

*Competencies are listed in order of their difference means. "Distance Education," the competency with the highest difference mean, appears at the top of the list; "Electronic Performance Support Systems," which has the second-highest difference mean, appears second; and so forth.

Competency Name [Competency Grouping]	Current Rank (Mean)	Future Rank (Mean)	Difference (Mean)
Goal Implementation [Leadership]	17 (3.75)	22 (4.18)	(+.43)
Group Dynamics [Leadership]	31 (3.54)	35 (3.96)	(+.42)
Ethics Modeling [Leadership]	26 (3.60)	34 (4.01)	(+.41)
Competency Identification [Analytical]	2 (4.13)	1 (4.52)	(+.39)
Project Management [Business]	19 (3.71)	27 (4.10)	(+.39)
Feedback [Technical]	6 (3.92)	15 (4.30)	(+.38)
Leadership [Leadership]	3 (4.10)	3 (4.48)	(+.38)
Model Building [Analytical]	47 (3.24)	50 (3.60)	(+.36)
Interpersonal Relationship Building [Interpersonal]	5 (3.97)	14 (4.32)	(+.35)
Analytical Thinking [Analytical]	4 (4.09)	6 (4.43)	(+.34)
Diversity Awareness [Leadership]	36 (3.44)	47 (3.78)	(+.34)
Facilitation [Technical]	12 (3.87)	20 (4.20)	(+.33)
Quality Implications [Business]	38 (3.40)	48 (3.72)	(+.32)
Adult Learning [Technical]	9 (3.91)	21 (4.19)	(+.28)
Questioning [Technical]	13 (3.87)	26 (4.15)	(+.28)
Communication [Interpersonal]	1 (4.17)	4 (4.44)	(+.27)
Training Theory and Application [Analytical]	23 (3.66)	39 (3.93)	(+.27)
Survey Design and Development [Technical]	46 (3.29)	52 (3.53)	(+.24)

These competencies represent the analytical, business, and technological competency groupings. Of the top 10 competencies on the current list, four are analytical competencies, two are interpersonal competencies, two are technical competencies, one is a business competency, one is a leadership competency, and none are technological competencies. Of the top 11 future competencies, five are in the analytical grouping, three are in the business grouping, three are in the leadership grouping, one is in the interpersonal grouping, and one is in the technological grouping. Note that "technological literacy" is the one technological competency that the practitioners selected. It is also the only technological competency that seems to focus inward on the practitioner, rather than outward on the organization. The other three technological competencies ("distance learning," "computer-mediated communication," and "electronic performance support systems") all suggest skills that the WLP practitioner will use to assist other employees of the organization in their learning and communication efforts.

WLP Expert Responses

Although the WLP experts are in the same field as the WLP practitioners, they offer a different viewpoint. Seasoned veterans, who tend to see the profession from a 30,000 foot view, compose this group. In addition, they tend to be well informed about best practices across the profession, and they tend to have a clear idea about the common issues that WLP professionals face in all types of industries. Although this viewpoint is not necessarily a reliable predictor of the future, it does validate the data from a more authoritative source than WLP practitioners or line managers. In no way does the study attempt to compare the accuracy of one group's responses against those of another group. Although understanding the different perceptions of each

Table 5.2: WLP Practitioners

Current: Top-Ranked Competencies			*Future:* Top-Ranked Competencies		
Rank	Competency	Mean	Rank	Competency	Mean
1	Communication	(4.17)	1	Competency Identification	(4.52)
2	Competency Identification	(4.13)	2	Technological Literacy	(4.51)
3	Leadership	(4.10)	3	Leadership	(4.48)
4	Analytical Thinking	(4.09)	*4	Communication	(4.44)
5	Interpersonal Relationship Building	(3.97)	*5	Intervention Selection	(4.44)
*6	Feedback	(3.92)	6	Analytical Thinking	(4.43)
*7	Intervention Selection	(3.92)	*7	Industry Awareness	(4.38)
*8	Industry Awareness	(3.92)	*8	Performance Gap Analysis	(4.38)
9	Adult Learning	(3.91)	9	Ability to See the "Big Picture"	(4.37)
10	Performance Gap Analysis	(3.90)	*10	Evaluation of Results Against Organizational Goals	(4.34)
			*11	Knowledge Management	(4.34)

*Indicates a tie. Either competency could be in the higher or lower ranking.

Note: An 11th ranking was added to the future side of this table, due to a tie for 10th place.

group is important, one cannot determine which group's predictions are more apt to be accurate.

The WLP expert group saw 51 of the 52 competencies increasing in importance over the next five years. They saw only "survey design and development" as remaining the same in future importance. The group indicated that 13 of these same competencies are likely to increase significantly (by more than 10 percent) in importance over the next five years. Table 5.3 uses the same labels as table 5.1 for all competencies, rankings, and mean scores.

◆ ◆ ◆

Although understanding the different perceptions of each group is important, one cannot determine which group's predictions are more apt to be accurate.

◆ ◆ ◆

Of the 13 competencies that the WLP experts identified as increasing significantly in importance in the future, five are analytical, four are business, and four are technological. The experts did not identify any of the technical, leadership, or interpersonal competencies as increasing significantly in importance in the future. Clearly the WLP experts feel that the future of the profession lies in a consultative role, but WLP practitioners feel that it lies in the role of helping organizations to link human performance to business goals. Analysis and an understanding of business results are two critical pieces of this HPI process. Many respondents predicted that technology will enable WLP practitioners to improve performance and streamline processes. Interestingly, the expert group saw far fewer of the 52 competencies increasing in importance in the future than did the WLP practitioner group (13 versus 22). Also, when given the opportunity to add any competencies that they felt were missing from the list, the experts identified only "creativity." They agreed on what the competencies will be for the future, but they felt that very few will be more important in five years than they are now. One way to explain this phenomenon is through mathematics. Overall, the experts placed slightly more weight on the current importance of the 52 competencies than the WLP practitioners did (3.69 versus 3.59). The experts felt that today's WLP practitioners already need to have many of these competencies. When it comes to future importance, however, the WLP practitioners and experts are nearly dead even (4.10 versus 4.11). Therefore, the difference in opinion comes down to timing, not importance. The two groups agree on the overall future value of devel-

oping these competencies. They only differ in their views on how urgent the acquisition of the competencies is and on what the required groupings of competencies will be.

The most remarkable increases in importance between current and future competencies predicted by expert respondents are

◆ knowledge management (+.88)
◆ computer-mediated communication (+.94)
◆ distance education (+1.06)
◆ electronic performance support systems (+.92)
◆ outsourcing management (+.90).

Top-10 Competency Rankings for the WLP -Expert Group
An examination of their top-ranked competencies provides more insight into the expert perspective. Table 5.4 uses the same labels and rules for understanding the rankings as table 5.2.

Three of the future competencies do not appear on the current side of the list. These three competencies are "technological literacy," "ability to see the 'big picture,'" and "knowledge management." These three competencies are the same ones that the WLP practitioner group identified as jumping into the limelight in the next five years. Note here that this increase is probably not caused by mathematical rounding off or random ranking of the ties. "Ability to see the 'big picture'" moved from 17th place to 10th place, requiring a difference score of +.48. "Technological literacy" jumped from 21st place and "knowledge management" jumped from 30th place, requiring remarkable difference scores of +.78 and +.88 respectively. These are among the largest increases in the entire study.

Of the competencies receiving the total top-10 current scores, three are analytical competencies, three are leadership competencies, two are interpersonal competencies, one is a technical competency, and one is a business competency. The experts did not place any of the technological competencies in their current top-10 ratings. Of the top-10 future competencies, three are analytical competencies, three are leadership competencies, two are business competencies, one is an interpersonal competency, and one is a technological competency. No technical competencies made the future list. Again, WLP experts consider analytical competencies extremely important. Clearly these competencies will be necessary to allow WLP practitioners to follow the HPI model. As mentioned previously, the WLP experts and practitioners both chose "technological literacy" as their sole technological competency represented in the top-10 future rankings. Comparing this to the top-10

Table 5.3: Expert Responses
Competency Rankings in Order of Difference*

Competency Name [Competency Grouping]	Current Rank (Mean)	Future Rank (Mean)	Mean Difference (Mean)
Distance Education [Technological]	49 (3.16)	24 (4.22)	(+1.06)
Computer-Mediated Communication [Technological]	42 (3.34)	17 (4.28)	(+.94)
Electronic Performance Support Systems [Technological]	50 (3.08)	34 (4.00)	(+.92)
Outsourcing Management [Business]	48 (3.16)	32 (4.06)	(+.90)
Knowledge Management [Analytical]	30 (3.64)	6 (4.52)	(+.88)
Technological Literacy [Technological]	21 (3.80)	2 (4.58)	(+.78)
Evaluation of Results Against Organizational Goals [Business]	37 (3.54)	18 (4.28)	(+.74)
Knowledge Capital [Business]	46 (3.22)	42 (3.88)	(+.66)
Cost/Benefit Analysis [Business]	41 (3.38)	35 (4.00)	(+.62)
Reward System Theory and Application [Analytical]	44 (3.32)	40 (3.92)	(+.60)
Systems Thinking [Analytical]	10 (4.04)	3 (4.58)	(+.54)
Analyzing Performance Data [Analytical]	38 (3.46)	37 (3.98)	(+.52)
Work Environment Analysis [Analytical]	35 (3.56)	31 (4.08)	(+.50)
Ability to See the "Big Picture" [Business]	17 (3.94)	10 (4.42)	(+.48)
Career Development Theory and Application [Analytical]	52 (2.90)	51 (3.38)	(+.48)
Intervention Selection [Analytical]	19 (3.80)	19 (4.28)	(+.48)

*Competencies are listed in order of their difference means. "Distance Education," the competency with the highest difference mean, appears at the top of the list; "computer-mediated communication," which has the second-highest difference mean, appears second; and so forth.

Competency Name [Competency Grouping]	Current Rank (Mean)	Future Rank (Mean)	Mean Difference (Mean)
Social Awareness [Analytical]	32 (3.60)	30 (4.08)	(+.48)
Performance Theory [Analytical]	34 (3.58)	33 (4.02)	(+.44)
Standards Identification [Analytical]	26 (3.68)	28 (4.12)	(+.44)
Negotiating/Contracting [Business]	40 (3.41)	43 (3.84)	(+.43)
Coping Skills [Interpersonal]	28 (3.66)	29 (4.08)	(+.42)
Ethics Modeling [Leadership]	20 (3.80)	23 (4.22)	(+.42)
Organization Development Theory and Application [Analytical]	36 (3.54)	39 (3.96)	(+.42)
Feedback [Technical]	18 (3.84)	22 (4.24)	(+.40)
Identification of Critical Business Issues [Business]	9 (4.12)	5 (4.52)	(+.40)
Staff Selection Theory and Application [Analytical]	47 (3.20)	48 (3.60)	(+.40)
Visioning [Leadership]	8 (4.12)	4 (4.52)	(+.40)
Communication Networks [Interpersonal]	31 (3.60)	38 (3.98)	(+.38)
Goal Implementation [Leadership]	14 (3.94)	15 (4.32)	(+.38)
Intervention Monitoring [Technical]	39 (3.42)	44 (3.80)	(+.38)
Process Consultation [Analytical]	25 (3.76)	25 (4.14)	(+.38)
Business Knowledge [Business]	11 (4.02)	12 (4.38)	(+.36)
Model Building [Analytical]	23 (3.78)	26 (4.14)	(+.36)

Competency Name [Competency Grouping]	Current Rank (Mean)	Future Rank (Mean)	Mean Difference (Mean)
Consulting [Interpersonal]	12 (4.00)	13 (4.34)	(+.34)
Industry Awareness [Business]	16 (3.94)	20 (4.28)	(+.34)
Buy-in/Advocacy [Leadership]	7 (4.14)	9 (4.46)	(+.32)
Workplace Performance, Learning Strategies, and Intervention Evaluation [Analytical]	15 (3.94)	21 (4.24)	(+.30)
Interpersonal Relationship Building [Interpersonal]	3 (4.24)	7 (4.52)	(+.28)
Leadership [Leadership]	2 (4.38)	1 (4.66)	(+.28)
Group Dynamics [Leadership]	24 (3.76)	36 (3.98)	(+.22)
Communication [Interpersonal]	5 (4.20)	11 (4.40)	(+.20)
Diversity Awareness [Leadership]	33 (3.58)	45 (3.76)	(+.18)
Performance Gap Analysis [Analytical]	6 (4.16)	14 (4.34)	(+.18)
Training Theory and Application [Analytical]	43 (3.34)	49 (3.52)	(+.18)
Competency Identification [Analytical]	13 (3.96)	27 (4.12)	(+.16)
Quality Implications [Business]	45 (3.24)	50 (3.39)	(+.15)
Facilitation [Technical]	4 (4.20)	16 (4.32)	(+.12)
Project Management [Business]	22 (3.78)	41 (3.90)	(+.12)
Questioning [Technical]	27 (3.68)	46 (3.76)	(+.08)

*Competencies are listed in order of their difference means. "Distance Education," the competency with the highest difference mean, appears at the top of the list; "computer-mediated communication," which has the second-highest difference mean, appears second; and so forth.

Competency Name [Competency Grouping]	Current Rank (Mean)	Future Rank (Mean)	Mean Difference (Mean)
Adult Learning [Technical]	29 (3.65)	47 (3.69)	(+.04)
Analytical Thinking [Analytical]	1 (4.44)	8 (4.48)	(+.04)
Survey Design and Development [Technical]	51 (3.02)	52 (3.02)	(0)

Table 5.4: Experts

Current: Top-Ranked Competencies

Rank	Competency	Mean
1	Analytical Thinking	(4.44)
2	Leadership	(4.38)
3	Interpersonal Relationship Building	(4.24)
*4	Facilitation	(4.20)
*5	Communication	(4.20)
6	Performance Gap Analysis	(4.16)
7	Buy-in/Advocacy	(4.14)
*8	Visioning	(4.12)
*9	Identification of Critical Business Issues	(4.12)
10	Systems Thinking	(4.04)

Future: Top-Ranked Competencies

Rank	Competency	Mean
1	Leadership	(4.66)
*2	Technological Literacy	(4.58)
*3	Systems Thinking	(4.58)
*4	Visioning	(4.52)
*5	Identification of Critical Business Issues	(4.52)
*6	Knowledge Management	(4.52)
*7	Interpersonal Relationship Building	(4.52)
8	Analytical Thinking	(4.48)
9	Buy-in/Advocacy	(4.46)
10	Ability to See the "Big Picture"	(4.42)

*Indicates a tie. Either competency could be in the higher or lower ranking.

rankings of the line managers uncovers a startling gap.

Line Manager Responses

The involvement of line managers in this study represents a radical departure from previous studies. Although they represent a very small sample of the total line manager population (31 total participants), they also present a vital perspective. Line managers are the primary recipients and sponsors of most WLP endeavors and, therefore, their expectations for WLP practitioners is important. Too often, service providers make false assumptions about the needs of their customers. This is the first competency study to step outside the profession and collect the opinions of those who view WLP services from a unique perspective. Future studies will need to collect more data from this group in order to substantiate these initial findings. This particular group of line managers turned out to be extremely experienced: 52 percent had over 16 years of management experience.

When asked if the list of 52 competencies "accurately represent those critical to the job success of workplace learning and performance professionals," 100 percent of the line managers responded "yes." One line manager wrote: "if the people who I dealt with in your profession had all of these skills, my job would be easy." The line manager group also saw 51 of the 52 competencies increasing in importance over the next five years. They viewed only "ethics modeling" as remain-

◆ ◆ ◆

Although technologies can offer a rapid return-on-investment (that is, time and cost savings), they do not offer the longer term benefits of other WLP interventions.

◆ ◆ ◆

ing the same in importance over the next five years. The line managers identified three of the 52 competencies as increasing significantly (by 10 percent or more) in importance over the next five years. In table 5.5, daggers identify these three competencies.

Surprisingly, the line managers identified no competencies from the analytical, technical, leadership, business, or interpersonal groupings as increasing significantly in importance in the future. They saw the importance of only three technological competencies increasing significantly in the future: "computer-mediated communication," "distance education," and "electronic performance support systems." These technological competencies focus outward on providing services to the organization, rather than inward on developing the skill and knowledge of the individual WLP practitioner. Unlike WLP practitioners, the line managers did not identify "technological literacy" as increasing significantly in importance in the future. This may indicate that line managers are assuming that WLP professionals should already have technological literacy and now need to move on to providing pervasive learning experiences for the entire organization via electronic means.

WLP professionals may be disconcerted, however, to see that the primary future role that line managers see for the WLP profession centers on learning and commu-

nication technologies. Although technologies can offer a rapid return-on-investment (that is, time and cost savings), they do not offer the longer term benefits of other WLP interventions. But the use of learning and communication technology has received a disproportionate amount of exposure in the press lately. Rarely does a business publication today not print several articles on the use of technology to speed up communication and educate the workforce. These publications are less likely to print articles about how innovative interventions such as job redesign, rewards and recognition policies, and process reengineering are improving human performance.

Top-10 Competency Rankings for Line Manager Group

Examination of the top-10 current and future competency rankings presents a clearer picture of the line manager's perspective. Because the only competencies with significant increases in mean are the three technological competencies mentioned earlier, many more competencies made both the current and future lists in the line manager group than in the other respondent groups. Without these significant increases in mean, fewer competencies could leapfrog onto the top-10 future list without first making the top-10 current list. "Computer-mediated communication" and "knowledge management" are the only two competencies that are on the top-10 future competencies list and are not also on the top-10 current list.

Comparisons Between the Groups

The exploration of the respondent group's data brought up some interesting comparisons between their responses. Although these comparisons help to make the data more meaningful, they only begin to scratch the surface of what the research revealed. The following information will further clarify what the research results determined about the various perceptions of the three respondent groups. Note that the study collected very little data about the root causes for these perceptions. Because these competencies represent a new body of knowledge, the focus was on validating them. The research design did not include a further exploration of the underlying causes for these differences in perception. Perhaps future studies will do so. Only the expert and line manager questionnaires asked the following qualitative questions:

◆ Do you believe that the competencies listed above accurately represent those critical to the job success

Table 5.5: Line Manager Responses
Competency Rankings in Order of Difference*

Competency Name [Competency Grouping]	Current Rank (Mean)	Future Rank (Mean)	Mean Difference (Mean)
†Computer-Mediated Communication [Technological]	22 (3.65)	6 (4.32)	(+.67)
†Distance Education [Technological]	44 (3.26)	22 (3.91)	(+.65)
†Electronic Performance Support Systems [Technological]	45 (3.22)	33 (3.73)	(+.51)
Technological Literacy [Technological]	23 (3.65)	15 (4.09)	(+.44)
Negotiating/Contracting [Business]	49 (3.17)	40 (3.59)	(+.42)
Knowledge Management [Analytical]	18 (3.78)	10 (4.18)	(+.40)
Knowledge Capital [Business]	39 (3.35)	31 (3.73)	(+.38)
Outsourcing Management [Business]	51 (3.00)	48 (3.36)	(+.36)
Analyzing Performance Data [Analytical]	37 (3.48)	29 (3.77)	(+.29)
Social Awareness [Analytical]	50 (3.09)	47 (3.38)	(+.29)
Workplace Performance, Learning Strategies, and Intervention Evaluation [Analytical]	27 (3.59)	25 (3.86)	(+.27)
Business Knowledge [Business]	21 (3.65)	20 (3.91)	(+.26)
Adult Learning [Technical]	36 (3.48)	32 (3.73)	(+.25)
Evaluation of Results Against Organizational Goals [Business]	33 (3.57)	27 (3.82)	(+.25)
Organization Development Theory and Application [Analytical]	43 (3.30)	42 (3.55)	(+.25)
Survey Design and Development [Technical]	42 (3.30)	43 (3.55)	(+.25)

*Competencies are listed in order of their difference means. "Computer-Mediated Communication," the competency with the highest difference mean, appears at the top of the list; "Distance Education," which has the second-highest difference mean, appears second; and so forth.

†Competencies that line managers identified as increasing significantly (by 10 percent or more) in importance over the next five years.

Competency Name [Competency Grouping]	Current Rank (Mean)	Future Rank (Mean)	Mean Difference (Mean)
Systems Thinking [Analytical]	30 (3.57)	26 (3.82)	(+.25)
Ability to See the "Big Picture" [Business]	4 (4.26)	2 (4.50)	(+.24)
Identification of Critical Business Issues [Business]	7 (4.14)	5 (4.38)	(+.24)
Leadership [Leadership]	3 (4.26)	1 (4.50)	(+.24)
Model Building [Analytical]	52 (2.86)	52 (3.10)	(+.24)
Industry Awareness [Business]	19 (3.74)	18 (3.96)	(+.22)
Communication Networks [Interpersonal]	24 (3.61)	28 (3.82)	(+.21)
Cost/Benefit Analysis [Business]	20 (3.65)	23 (3.86)	(+.21)
Coping Skills [Interpersonal]	32 (3.57)	30 (3.77)	(+.20)
Intervention Monitoring [Technical]	48 (3.17)	50 (3.36)	(+.19)
Project Management [Business]	13 (3.96)	14 (4.14)	(+.18)
Consulting [Interpersonal]	31 (3.57)	34 (3.73)	(+.16)
Diversity Awareness [Leadership]	40 (3.32)	44 (3.48)	(+.16)
Staff Selection Theory and Application [Analytical]	35 (3.52)	36 (3.68)	(+.16)
Training Theory and Application [Analytical]	41 (3.30)	45 (3.46)	(+.16)
Analytical Thinking [Analytical]	8 (4.13)	7 (4.27)	(+.14)
Goal Implementation [Leadership]	11 (4.00)	13 (4.14)	(+.14)

*Competencies are listed in order of their difference means. "Computer-Mediated Communication," the competency with the highest difference mean, appears at the top of the list; "Distance Education," which has the second-highest difference mean, appears second; and so forth.

Competency Name [Competency Grouping]	Current Rank (Mean)	Future Rank (Mean)	Mean Difference (Mean)
Quality Implications [Business]	46 (3.22)	49 (3.36)	(+.14)
Interpersonal Relationship Building [Interpersonal]	10 (4.04)	12 (4.18)	(+.14)
Buy-in/Advocacy [Leadership]	24 (3.91)	17 (4.00)	(+.09)
Facilitation [Technical]	16 (3.87)	19 (3.96)	(+.09)
Performance Gap Analysis [Analytical]	9 (4.09)	11 (4.18)	(+.09)
Process Consultation [Analytical]	25 (3.61)	35 (3.68)	(+.07)
Questioning [Technical]	26 (3.61)	37 (3.68)	(+.07)
Reward System Theory and Application [Analytical]	34 (3.52)	39 (3.59)	(+.07)
Work Environment Analysis [Analytical]	28 (3.57)	38 (3.64)	(+.07)
Intervention Selection [Analytical]	2 (4.35)	4 (4.41)	(+.06)
Communication [Interpersonal]	6 (4.17)	8 (4.23)	(+.06)
Performance Theory [Analytical]	38 (3.35)	46 (3.41)	(+.06)
Standards Identification [Analytical]	5 (4.17)	9 (4.23)	(+.06)
Group Dynamics [Leadership]	47 (3.22)	51 (3.27)	(+.05)
Feedback [Technical]	12 (3.96)	16 (4.00)	(+.04)
Visioning [Leadership]	17 (3.83)	24 (3.86)	(+.03)
Career Development Theory and Application [Analytical]	29 (3.57)	41 (3.59)	(+.02)

Table 5.5: Line Manager Responses
Competency Rankings in Order of Difference* (continued)

Competency Name [Competency Grouping]	Current Rank (Mean)	Future Rank (Mean)	Mean Difference (Mean)
Competency Identification [Analytical]	1 (4.44)	3 (4.46)	(+.02)
Ethics Modeling [Leadership]	15 (3.91)	21 (3.91)	(0)

*Competencies are listed in order of their difference means. "Computer-Mediated Communication," the competency with the highest difference mean, appears at the top of the list; "Distance Education," which has the second-highest difference mean, appears second; and so forth.

Table 5.6: Line Managers

Current: Top-Ranked Competencies			*Future:* Top-Ranked Competencies		
Rank	Competency	Mean	Rank	Competency	Mean
1	Competency Identification	(4.44)	*1	Leadership	(4.50)
2	Intervention Selection	(4.35)	*2	Ability to See the "Big Picture"	(4.50)
*3	Leadership	(4.26)	3	Competency Identification	(4.46)
*4	Ability to See the "Big Picture"	(4.26)	4	Intervention Selection	(4.41)
*5	Standards Identification	(4.17)	5	Identification of Critical Business Issues	(4.38)*
6	Communication	(4.17)	6	Computer Mediated Communication	(4.32)
7	Identification of Critical Business Issues	(4.14)	7	Analytical Thinking	(4.27)
8	Analytical Thinking	(4.13)	*8	Communication	(4.23)
9	Performance Gap Analysis	(4.09)	*9	Standards Identification	(4.23)
10	Interpersonal Relationship Building	(4.04)	*10	Knowledge Management	(4.18)
			*11	Performance Gap Analysis	(4.18)
			*12	Interpersonal Relationship Building	(4.18)

*Indicates a tie. Either competency could be in the higher or lower ranking.

Note: Due to a tie for 10th place, 11th and 12th rankings were added to the future side of this table.

of workplace learning and performance professionals? Why or why not?

◆ Please identify any specific competencies critical to the job success of workplace learning and performance professionals, either now or in the future, that are not listed above.

◆ Please identify what you consider to be the significant future trends in the American workplace that will most profoundly affect the role and/or job success of workplace learning and performance professionals over the next five years.

◆ What do you foresee as the primary role(s) of workplace learning and performance over the next five years? Why?

The first two questions ask about the competencies that were or were not included in the study. As stated earlier, the overwhelming consensus of the WLP experts and line managers was that the study did include all of the major competencies needed for WLP work. The responses to the third and fourth questions relate most directly to the root causes for differing perceptions of the future. Both of these questions specifically ask for insight on the future of the WLP profession. Much of the discussion that follows deals with responses to these questions.

Table 5.7 displays the various mean scores achieved within each competency grouping (that is, analytical, technical, leadership, business, interpersonal, and technological). Adding together all of the mean scores for the competencies within the competency grouping and dividing by the number of items within that grouping gives the mean score for a competency grouping. For instance, four of the 52 competencies are technological

Table 5.7: Competency Groupings: Means by Respondent Group

Group	Total Current and Future	Analytical	Technical	Leadership	Business	Inter-personal	Techno-logical
WLP Practitioner	C=3.59 F=4.10 D=.51*	C=3.56 F=4.07 D=.51*	C=3.72 F=4.06 D=.34	C=3.71 F=4.13 D=.42	C=3.49 F=4.04 D=.55*	C=3.77 F=4.20 D=.43	C=3.43 F=4.25 D=.82**
Expert	C=3.69 F=4.11 D=.42	C=3.67 F=4.08 D=.41	C=3.64 F=3.81 D=.17	C=3.96 F=4.27 D=.31	C=3.61 F=4.09 D=.48	C=3.94 F=4.26 D=.32	C=3.35 F=4.27 D=.92**
Line Manager	C=3.65 F=3.85 D=.20	C=3.65 F=3.80 D=.15	C=3.57 F=3.71 D=.14	C=3.78 F=3.88 D=.10	C=3.61 F=3.87 D=.26	C=3.79 F=3.95 D=.16	C=3.45 F=4.01 D=.56*
Total Average	C=3.64 F=4.02 D=.38	C=3.63 F=3.98 D=.35	C=3.64 F=3.86 D=.22	C=3.82 F=4.09 D=.27	C=3.57 F=4.00 D=.43	C=3.83 F=4.14 D=.31	C=3.41 F=4.18 D=.77**

"Total Current & Future" (column one) = Average of all 52 competencies within a respondent group, added together and divided by the total number of competencies (52).

"C"= [current] Average, mean score of all *current* competencies within a competency grouping, divided by the number of competencies within the grouping.

"F"= [future] Average, mean score of all *future* competencies within a competency grouping, divided by the number of competencies within the grouping.

"D"= (Difference) The future score minus the current score within each cell.

"Total Average" (row) = The current or future competency grouping average of all three respondent groups, added together and then divided by three. The difference scores in this row are calculated within the cell.

*= Significant increase of above 10% (>.50) between current and future scores.

**= Significant increase of above 15% (>.75) between current and future scores.

competencies ("distance learning," "computer communication," "electronic performance support systems," and "computer-mediated learning"). Each of these competencies has a current and future mean score for each respondent group. Adding these four scores together and then dividing by four (that is, the number of competencies in the grouping) determines a mean score for the category. In essence, the grouping score is a "mean of means." This information is useful because it allows one to draw comparisons between the types of competencies that each respondent group saw as growing in importance over the next five years. Although it may be overwhelming to consider the relative importance of each of the 52 competencies for the three respondent groups (that is, WLP practitioners, experts, and line managers) it may be revealing to compare each respondent group's assessment of the six competency groupings. Note that respondents were not aware of the existence of competency groupings. Furthermore, the competencies did not appear on the questionnaire in any particular order. Therefore, the organization of the survey instrument almost certainly did not influence the responses. No evidence suggests that items at the end of the survey instrument were more or less likely to receive a certain rating than items at the beginning of the instrument.

The difference between the current and future scores (noted as "D=") shows the average amount of increase that the respondent groups reported within each competency grouping. An asterisk notes any difference that exceeds .50 (which is at least a 10 percent increase). Although these differences may not be statistically significant, they do show a clear increase in the expectation for future work in this area.

Table 5.7 displays some important points. Although the total current scores of all three groups are close (3.59, 3.69, and 3.65), the amount of increase between the groups is considerably different. The WLP practitioner group saw the average competency increasing in importance by over 10 percent (+.51), the WLP expert group was close behind, predicting an average increase in importance of 8 percent (+.42), and the line manager group saw an increase in importance of only 4 percent (.20) overall for the competencies. This is less than half of what either of the professional WLP groups saw.

These data raise an interesting question: Why do line managers not see the same amount of increase in importance that the WLP groups see? Although the study collected no specific data on this question, plenty of anecdotal evidence suggests that the line managers believe that WLP professionals should already have

these competencies. Although the quantitative current averages are all fairly close, they may not show the whole picture. In the qualitative questions, however, numerous statements provide greater insight into this question. When given the opportunity to elaborate on their responses, line managers did agree that the questionnaire provided a comprehensive list of WLP competencies. When asked to list any missing competencies, line managers frequently suggested competencies like "rapid adaptability," "keeping pace with the rate of change," and "quickly learning about new information." Although these are more perspectives than competencies, they do indicate that speed is an essential component of the line managers' world. We may assume, then, that line managers would expect WLP professionals to conform to this rapid pace. The WLP practitioners and WLP experts seemed to have no problem accepting the notion that the "future" label on the questionnaire described "five years from now." For many line managers, however, the "future" is not much further away than tomorrow. Therefore, the WLP professional must adjust his or her perspective of the future to align with the line manager's perspective. To do so, WLP professionals must increase the pace at which they understand and adapt to the new reality of today's marketplace. One cannot overstate that success in an information-age business depends heavily on speed, and WLP professionals must meet this need if they are to continue having a positive effect on organizations.

All three groups saw the most significant increase in importance occurring in technological competencies. Although the line managers did not see these competencies increasing as dramatically as the WLP experts and practitioners did, they averaged an amazing increase overall of .77 (over 15 percent). The WLP practitioners are the only ones who saw significant increases occurring in the analytical and business competency groupings. Certain competencies within these two groupings drive the overall difference. The analytical competency grouping showed significant differences in the competency ratings (that is, the differences in the amount of increase in importance between current and future competencies of the three respondent groups) of "performance gap analysis," "analytical thinking," and "competency identification." In each of these cases, the WLP practitioners saw at least twice as much increase in current versus future importance as the expert and line manager groups. Several of the other analytical competencies showed similar gaps between the WLP practitioner and line manager difference scores. In some cases, the WLP practitioners saw 10 to 20 times more of an increase in importance than the line managers saw. For example, intervention selection (.52 versus .06), reward system theory and application (.54 versus .07), and career development theory (.52 versus .02). In general, the expert ratings are similar to the WLP practitioner ratings for those competencies that show a huge gap between WLP practitioner and line manager ratings.

In the business competency grouping, all of the competencies (except for "negotiating/contracting") had large gaps between the line manager and WLP practitioner difference scores. The difference scores of the experts tended to be more in line with those of the WLP practitioners, except in the case of "project management" and "quality implications." For these two competencies, the WLP practitioner ratings are at least double those of the experts and line managers. Note also that the expert group rated "evaluation of results against organizational goals" and "outsourcing management" higher than the other two respondent groups did. In every other case within this grouping, the WLP practitioners consistently gave the highest difference score.

Table 5.8 provides a comparison of the difference scores for the remaining competency groupings. Although relatively large gaps separate respondent group ratings in some of the individual competencies in the leadership, technical, and interpersonal competency groupings, the difference is not significant when averaged together with the other competencies in that grouping.

Combined Rankings and Means of Groups
In order to gauge differences between the respondent groups' rankings, one needs composite measures against which to benchmark them. Table 5.9 provides just such composite measures. Adding the current and future competency scores for all three respondent groups and then dividing by three created the information for this table. For example:

Performance Gap Analysis [current]:

3.90 (practitioner group's mean) + 4.16 (expert group's mean) + 4.09 (line manager group's mean) = 12.15 (total) ÷ 3 (total number of respondent groups) = 4.05

Top-10 Competencies of the Three Groups Combined
Although comparing each of the respondent group's competency averages against the combined average scores is not practical or particularly interesting, examining the top-10 combined rankings may help guide

people in their development plans. Table 5.10 shows the combined rankings with their means.

No major gaps appear between these combined group rankings and those of the individual respondent groups because these scores are an average of the respondent group scores. However, these scores show how much above or below the average any one score is. This table gives one of the most complete views of the future one can create with the data available. Notice that eight out of the top 10 ranked competencies appear on both the current and future sides of the chart. Also notice that "leadership" is in the number one position in both the current and future rankings.

Competencies on the Top-10 List in Each of the Three Groups
Some competencies appeared in the top-10 lists of all three respondent groups. If one were to lay tables 5.2, 5.4, and 5.6 side by side, the following competencies would appear in each of those tables and in the same time frame (that is, current or future): under current, leadership, communication, analytical thinking, performance gap analysis, and interpersonal relationship building; and under future, leadership, ability to see the "big picture," and analytical thinking. This juxtaposition demonstrates how three groups independently of each other recognized many of the same patterns. These patterns provide some of the strongest insights into the perceptions of WLP professionals and those who benefit from WLP services. Note that none of the means for each of the following competencies for the respondent groups have a significant difference (that is, .50 or greater). In fact, the differences are rather minimal or nonexistent in most cases.

When it comes to the future importance of the competencies, the line managers did not see the magnitude of change that the WLP experts and practitioners saw. Although all three groups have very similar mean scores for the combined 52 current competencies (practitioners: 3.59; experts: 3.69; line managers: 3.65), the gap grows considerably wider when comparing the future scores (practitioners: 4.10; experts: 4.11, line managers: 3.85). Subtracting the current means from the future means for each group causes the differences to become even more noticeable. The difference for WLP practitioners is +.51, for experts is +.42, and for the line managers is a scant +.20. The difference score for line managers is less than half that of either of the other group's scores. The reasons for this gap are difficult to identify. To begin with, the results do not suggest that the line managers feel the competencies are not important. In fact, in the current time frame, line

Table 5.8: A Comparison of Difference Scores for the Analytical, Business, Technical, Leadership, Interpersonal, and Technological Competencies

Analytical Competencies	Practitioner (difference scores)	Expert (difference scores)	Line Manager (difference scores)
Analytical Thinking	.34	.04	.14
Analyzing Performance Data	.57	.52	.29
Career Development Theory and Application	.52	.48	.02
Competency Identification	.39	.16	.02
Intervention Selection	.52	.48	.06
Knowledge Management	.80	.88	.40
Model Building	.36	.36	.24
Organization Development Theory and Application	.45	.42	.25
Performance Gap Analysis	.48	.18	.09
Performance Theory	.45	.44	.06
Process Consultation	.48	.38	.07
Reward System Theory and Application	.54	.60	.07
Social Awareness	.49	.48	.29
Staff Selection Theory and Application	.46	.40	.16
Standards Identification	.44	.44	.06
Systems Thinking	.69	.54	.25
Training Theory and Application	.27	.18	.16
Work Environment Analysis	.58	.50	.07
Workplace Performance, Learning Strategies, and Intervention Evaluation	.44	.30	.27
Mean Average for Analytical Competency Grouping	C=3.56 F=4.07 D=.51*	C=3.67 F=4.08 D=.41	C=3.65 F=3.80 D=.15

"C"= [current] Average, mean score of all *current* competencies within a competency grouping, divided by the number of competencies within the grouping.

"F"= [future] Average, mean score of all *future* competencies within a competency grouping, divided by the number of competencies within the grouping.

"D"= (Difference) The future score minus the current score within each cell.

*= Significant increase of above 10% (>.50) between current and future scores.

Business Competencies	Practitioner (difference scores)	Expert (difference scores)	Line Manager (difference scores)
Ability to See the "Big Picture"	.63	.48	.24
Business Knowledge	.54	.36	.26
Cost/Benefit Analysis	.63	.62	.21
Evaluation of Results Against Organizational Goals	.65	.74	.25
Identification of Critical Business Issues	.57	.40	.24
Industry Awareness	.46	.34	.22
Knowledge Capital	.70	.66	.38
Negotiating/Contracting	.48	.43	.42
Outsourcing Management	.69	.90	.36
Project Management	.39	.12	.18
Quality Implications	.32	.15	.14
Mean Average for Business Competency Grouping	C=3.49 F=4.04 D=.55*	C=3.61 F=4.09 D=.48	C=3.61 F=3.87 D=.26
Technical Competencies	Practitioner (difference scores)	Expert (difference scores)	Line Manager (difference scores)
Adult Learning	.28	.04	.25
Facilitation	.33	.12	.09
Feedback	.38	.40	.04
Intervention Monitoring	.51	.38	.19
Questioning	.28	.08	.07
Survey Design and Development	.24	0	.25
Mean Average for Technical Competency Grouping	C=3.72 F=4.06 D=.34	C=3.64 F=3.81 D=.17	C=3.57 F=3.71 D=.14
Leadership Competencies	Practitioner (difference scores)	Expert (difference scores)	Line Manager (difference scores)
Buy-in/Advocacy	.43	.32	.09
Diversity Awareness	.34	.18	.16

Table 5.8: A Comparison of Difference Scores for the Analytical, Business, Technical, Leadership, Interpersonal, and Technological Competencies (continued)

Leadership Competencies (continued)	Practitioner (difference scores)	Expert (difference scores)	Line Manager (difference scores)
Ethics Modeling	.41	.42	0
Goal Implementation	.43	.38	.14
Group Dynamics	.42	.22	.05
Leadership	.38	.28	.24
Visioning	.53	.40	.03
Mean Average for Leadership Competency Grouping	C=3.71 F=4.13 D=.42	C=3.96 F=4.27 D=.31	C=3.78 F=3.88 D=.10

Interpersonal Competencies	Practitioner (difference scores)	Expert (difference scores)	Line Manager (difference scores)
Communication	.27	.20	.06
Communication Networks	.50	.38	.21
Consulting	.53	.34	.16
Coping Skills	.49	.42	.20
Interpersonal Relationship Building	.35	.28	.14
Mean Average for Interpersonal Competency Grouping	C=3.77 F=4.20 D=.43	C=3.94 F=4.26 D=.32	C=3.79 F=3.95 D=.16

Technological Competencies	Practitioner (difference scores)	Expert (difference scores)	Line Manager (difference scores)
Computer-Mediated Communication	.75	.94	.67
Distance Education	.97	1.06	.65
Electronic Performance Support Systems	.88	.92	.51
Technological Literacy	.71	.78	.44
Mean Average for Technological Competency Grouping	C=3.43 F=4.25 D=.82**	C=3.35 F=4.27 D=.92**	C=3.45 F=4.01 D=.56*

"C"= [current] Average, mean score of all *current* competencies within a competency grouping, divided by the number of competencies within the grouping.

"F"= [future] Average, mean score of all *future* competencies within a competency grouping, divided by the number of competencies within the grouping.

"D"= (Difference) The future score minus the current score within each cell.

*= Significant increase of above 10% (>.50) between current and future scores.

Table 5.9: Responses of All Groups Combined
Competency Rankings in Order of Difference*

Competency Name [Competency Grouping]	Current Rank (Mean)	Future Rank (Mean)	Mean Difference (Mean)
Distance Education [Technological]	48 (3.21)	24 (4.10)	(+.89)
Computer-Mediated Communication [Technological]	31 (3.52)	11 (4.31)	(+.79)
Electronic Performance Support Systems [Technological]	51 (3.14)	33 (3.91)	(+.77)
Knowledge Management [Analytical]	26 (3.65)	9 (4.35)	(+.70)
Outsourcing Management [Business]	52 (3.10)	41 (3.75)	(+.65)
Technological Literacy [Technological]	20 (3.75)	5 (4.39)	(+.64)
Analyzing Performance Data [Analytical]	41 (3.37)	29 (3.98)	(+.61)
Knowledge Capital [Business]	50 (3.16)	43 (3.74)	(+.58)
Evaluation of Results Against Organizational Goals [Business]	29 (3.60)	21 (4.15)	(+.55)
Cost/Benefit Analysis [Business]	36 (3.45)	32 (3.94)	(+.49)
Systems Thinking [Analytical]	25 (3.67)	20 (4.16)	(+.49)
Ability to See the "Big Picture" [Business]	10 (3.98)	2 (4.43)	(+.45)
Negotiating/Contracting [Business]	43 (3.31)	40 (3.75)	(+.44)
Social Awareness [Analytical]	47 (3.26)	46 (3.68)	(+.42)
Identification of Critical Business Issues [Business]	8 (3.99)	4 (4.39)	(+.40)
Reward System Theory and Application [Analytical]	40 (3.38)	39 (3.78)	(+.40)
Work Environment Analysis [Analytical]	33 (3.50)	34 (3.89)	(+.39)

*Competencies are listed in order of their difference means. "Distance Education," the competency with the highest difference mean, appears at the top of the list; "Computer-Mediated Communication," which has the second-highest difference mean, appears second; and so forth.

Competency Name [Competency Grouping]	Current Rank (Mean)	Future Rank (Mean)	Mean Difference (Mean)
Business Knowledge [Business]	22 (3.72)	23 (4.10)	(+.38)
Coping Skills [Interpersonal]	30 (3.59)	31 (3.96)	(+.37)
Organization Development Theory and Application [Analytical]	38 (3.41)	38 (3.78)	(+.37)
Communication Networks [Interpersonal]	28 (3.62)	28 (3.98)	(+.36)
Intervention Monitoring [Technical]	42 (3.35)	45 (3.71)	(+.36)
Intervention Selection [Analytical]	7 (4.02)	6 (4.38)	(+.36)
Consulting [Interpersonal]	23 (3.69)	27 (4.04)	(+.35)
Career Development Theory and Application [Analytical]	46 (3.27)	50 (3.61)	(+.34)
Industry Awareness [Business]	16 (3.87)	15 (4.21)	(+.34)
Staff Selection Theory and Application [Analytical]	39 (3.38)	44 (3.72)	(+.34)
Workplace Performance, Learning Strategies, and Intervention Evaluation [Analytical]	18 (3.81)	22 (4.14)	(+.33)
Model Building [Analytical]	44 (3.29)	49 (3.61)	(+.32)
Standards Identification [Analytical]	14 (3.88)	16 (4.20)	(+.32)
Visioning [Leadership]	15 (3.88)	17 (4.20)	(+.32)
Goal Implementation [Leadership]	13 (3.90)	14 (4.21)	(+.31)
Performance Theory [Analytical]	34 (3.47)	37 (3.78)	(+.31)

*Competencies are listed in order of their difference means. "Distance Education," the competency with the highest difference mean, appears at the top of the list; "Computer-Mediated Communication," which has the second-highest difference mean, appears second; and so forth.

Competency Name [Competency Grouping]	Current Rank (Mean)	Future Rank (Mean)	Mean Difference (Mean)
Process Consultation [Analytical]	27 (3.65)	30 (3.96)	(+.31)
Leadership [Leadership]	1 (4.25)	1 (4.55)	(+.30)
Buy-in/Advocacy [Leadership]	11 (3.96)	13 (4.24)	(+.28)
Ethics Modeling [Leadership]	19 (3.77)	26 (4.05)	(+.28)
Feedback [Technical]	12 (3.91)	18 (4.18)	(+.27)
Interpersonal Relationship Building [Interpersonal]	5 (4.08)	10 (4.34)	(+.26)
Performance Gap Analysis [Analytical]	6 (4.05)	12 (4.30)	(+.25)
Group Dynamics [Leadership]	32 (3.51)	42 (3.74)	(+.23)
Project Management [Business]	17 (3.82)	25 (4.05)	(+.23)
Diversity Awareness [Leadership]	35 (3.45)	47 (3.67)	(+.22)
Training Theory and Application [Analytical]	37 (3.43)	48 (3.64)	(+.21)
Quality Implications [Business]	45 (3.29)	51 (3.49)	(+.20)
Adult Learning [Technical]	24 (3.68)	35 (3.87)	(+.19)
Competency Identification [Analytical]	3 (4.18)	7 (4.37)	(+.19)
Communication [Interpersonal]	4 (4.18)	8 (4.36)	(+.18)
Facilitation [Technical]	9 (3.98)	19 (4.16)	(+.18)
Analytical Thinking [Analytical]	2 (4.22)	3 (4.39)	(+.17)

Table 5.9: Responses of All Groups Combined
Competency Rankings in Order of Difference* (continued)

Competency Name [Competency Grouping]	Current Rank (Mean)	Future Rank (Mean)	Mean Difference (Mean)
Survey Design and Development [Technical]	49 (3.20)	52 (3.37)	(+.17)
Questioning [Technical]	21 (3.72)	36 (3.86)	(+.14)

*Competencies are listed in order of their difference means. "Distance Education," the competency with the highest difference mean, appears at the top of the list; "Computer-Mediated Communication," which has the second-highest difference mean, appears second; and so forth.

Table 5.10: All Groups Combined

Current: Top-Ranked Competencies

Rank	Competency	Mean
1	Leadership [Leadership]	(4.25)
2	Analytical Thinking [Analytical]	(4.22)
*3	Competency Identification [Analytical]	(4.18)
*4	Communication [Interpersonal]	(4.18)
5	Interpersonal Relationship Building [Interpersonal]	(4.08)
ᵛ6	Performance Gap Analysis [Analytical]	(4.05)
7	Intervention Selection [Analytical]	(4.02)
8	Identification of Critical Business Issues [Business]	(3.99)
ᵛ*9	Facilitation [Technical]	(3.98)
*10	Ability to See the "Big Picture" [Business]	(3.98)

Future: Top-Ranked Competencies

Rank	Competency	Mean
1	Leadership [Leadership]	(4.55)
2	Ability to See the "Big Picture" [Business]	(4.43)
*3	Analytical Thinking [Analytical]	(4.39)
*4	Identification of Critical Business Issues [Business]	(4.39)
ᵛ*5	Technological Literacy [Technological]	(4.39)
6	Intervention Selection [Analytical]	(4.38)
7	Competency Identification [Analytical]	(4.37)
8	Communication [Interpersonal]	(4.36)
ᵛ9	Knowledge Management [Analytical]	(4.35)
10	Interpersonal Relationship Building [Interpersonal]	(4.34)

*Indicates a tie. Either competency could be in the higher or lower ranking.

ᵛIndicates competencies that didn't appear in both the current and future list.

managers rated the combined 52 competencies higher in importance than the WLP practitioners did (3.65 versus 3.59). Line managers also had the opportunity to write in any competencies that they felt were missing from the questionnaire. In almost all cases, the line managers felt that the major competencies had been captured and offered very few additional competencies. Those offered appeared to be alternative descriptions for existing competencies and were not added to this study.

A plausible explanation for this gap is that line managers are not fully aware of the total range of services that WLP practitioners can offer and of the impact that these services can have on the organization. A study of the qualitative data listed in appendix A shows that many of the line managers still see the future role of WLP as the administration of training, recruitment, employee relations, and human resource policy. No data strongly suggest that the line managers see WLP professionals acting as true business partners who help them to solve performance problems. Only a few line managers mentioned that WLP professionals might help them to improve human performance by "using holistic and systematic approaches that solve problems."

Section Summary

This section summarized the data received from the three respondent groups: WLP practitioners, WLP ex-perts, and line managers. This section first explored each group's responses separately and then compared and contrasted their responses. In general, the study shows considerable agreement on the current emphasis placed on the competencies, but shows that the line managers differ considerably from the other groups in the amount of future importance they placed on the competencies in the next five years. This section also compared the combined difference scores for each com-petency grouping in order to gain a better sense of which types of competencies each respondent group tended to value. Table 5.7 demonstrates that technolog-ical competencies are the only ones all three groups ex-pected to increase significantly in importance. The WLP practitioner group, however, also saw the impor-tance of analytical and business competencies as in-creasing significantly in the future.

Most important, this section helped the readers to begin to answer the following questions for themselves:

◆ How different or similar were the perspectives of the three respondent groups?
◆ What types of skills do line managers expect WLP professionals to have in the near future?
◆ How well equipped are people in the WLP profes-sion for meeting these expectations?
◆ What types of competencies (that is, analytical, technical, leadership, technological, business, or in-terpersonal) should a WLP professional begin devel-oping immediately?

This section defines key terms associated with ethics and explains why ethical issues are important to WLP practitioners. This section also reviews potential ethical breaches stemming from WLP work and from trends affecting WLP. Finally, this section offers five strategies for resolving ethical challenges in WLP.

Defining Key Terms Associated With Ethics

Professional ethics have captured national and international attention as a result of an increasing number of ethical scandals in business and politics. *Ethics* is a term derived from the Latin word for character and refers to socially held principles of right and wrong. Most commonly, *ethics* refers to a system of moral principles or values that govern a profession, an occupation, or an industry. In order to fully understand ethics, one must have an accurate understanding of morals and values. *Morals* refer to knowing and applying the principles of right and wrong. *Values* refer to the core set of beliefs of an individual or a group.

Ethical breaches occur when people fail to live up to their moral principles. This may occur due to unscrupulous behavior or the collision of two or more conflicting values, and a person must choose the lesser of two evils. In an attempt to provide overall guidance, organizations often express ethics, morals, and values in codes of ethics or conduct that clarify expectations about the appropriate behavior of employees and associates of the organization.

The Importance of Ethical Issues to Those Charged With WLP Responsibilities

Ethics are important to WLP practitioners for several reasons. One reason is that ethical issues arise in many areas of WLP work. In *Models for HRD Practice* (McLagan, 1989), ASTD identifies 13 ethical issues for HRD work. These ethical issues are

1. maintaining appropriate confidentiality
2. saying "no" to inappropriate requests
3. showing respect for copyrights, sources, and intellectual property
4. ensuring truth in claims, data, and recommendations
5. balancing organizational and individual needs and interests
6. ensuring customer and user involvement, participation, and ownership
7. avoiding conflicts of interest

8. managing personal biases
9. showing respect for, interest in, and representation of individual and population differences
10. making the intervention appropriate to the customer's or user's needs
11. being sensitive to the direct and indirect effects of interventions and acting to address negative consequences
12. pricing or costing products or services fairly
13. using power appropriately (McLagan, 1989).

All of these ethical issues continue to apply to WLP work.

A 1995 research study by Rothwell and Cookson determined that most ethical breaches encountered in the field focus on four major areas:

1. turning "institutional initiatives to personal gain"
2. using "self-interested actions to sway institutional actions"
3. intentionally misrepresenting "information, program descriptions, or attendance" numbers
4. exhibiting "unusual or undesirable personal behavior" (Rothwell & Cookson, 1997).

A second reason that ethical issues are important to WLP work is that WLP practitioners often lead organizational efforts to establish and implement codes of ethics. Therefore, WLP practitioners must set a positive example of ethical behavior. A third reason is that an organization's reputation is a key asset in the marketplace. Ethical practices help the organization to gain a reputation with their customers for reliability and honesty. Without this reputation, organizations cannot survive for long.

Ethical Dilemmas That Arise in WLP Work

WLP practitioners may encounter situations that have a high potential for ethical breaches. These situations can arise from many facets of WLP work and from trends affecting WLP. These breaches are important for WLP practitioners to understand. Practitioners can best view them in the context of the HPI model. Recall that the steps in the HPI process include *performance analysis, cause analysis, intervention selection, intervention implementation, change management,* and *evaluation.* The following discussion describes the relationship between the HPI model and situations that can cause ethical breaches.

Performance Analysis

Performance analysts identify gaps between desired performance levels and actual performance levels. Possible ethical breaches in performance analysis include:

◆ choosing not to conduct a proper performance analysis in order to satisfy the client's request for an immediate intervention
◆ conducting performance analysis improperly by bending to undue pressure from executives or other stakeholders, with the result of knowingly misidentifying performance problems
◆ not advising clients when the desired level of performance they seek is completely unreasonable based on industry benchmarks.

The causes of such ethical breaches may stem from a lack of experience or an overwhelming desire to secure work from the client. Misidentifying the performance problems leads to an inability to determine what interventions would be appropriate and effective.

Cause Analysis

During cause analysis, WLP practitioners attempt to isolate the root causes of performance problems (that is, the cause for the gap between the desired level of performance and the actual level of performance). Possible ethical breaches that may arise during this analysis are

◆ deciding not to conduct a cause analysis because the underlying causes seem too ambiguous or complex
◆ knowingly attributing a problem to the wrong root causes
◆ improperly manipulating data to show the need for a certain intervention when the data do not support that need
◆ not acknowledging an awareness of misidentified root causes.

Such ethical breaches may be the result of a lack of expertise, a willingness to bend to undue and inappropriate influence exerted by others, or a conflict of interest in which WLP practitioners stand to gain or lose financially based on the results of their analysis. The likely consequences are an improper identification of the root causes and a resultant improper determination of appropriate interventions.

Intervention Selection

During intervention selection, WLP practitioners consider appropriate ways to solve performance problems.

The following ethical breaches are possible during this phase:

◆ knowingly selecting the wrong intervention because the WLP practitioner lacks the ability to implement the appropriate intervention (for example, selecting training when the cause analysis revealed a compensation issue as the root cause of a performance problem)
◆ selecting a particular intervention primarily because it best benefits the WLP practitioner
◆ selecting an intervention with the primary objective of developing the WLP practitioner's skill level
◆ yielding to a desire for unrealistic quick fixes or ineffective quick results
◆ consciously building unrealistic expectations among stakeholders about the time and resources needed to implement the appropriate intervention and to reach desired performance objectives.

A lack of expertise, a willingness to bend to undue client pressure, and a WLP practitioner's own greed can cause these ethical breaches. The likely consequences are a failed intervention, unnecessary expense, and an increased performance gap.

Intervention Implementation

The implementation phase puts interventions into practice. Possible ethical breaches during this phase include:

◆ failing to monitor the intervention's progress because there are no fees directly associated with this activity
◆ intentionally ignoring certain stakeholders because of their opposition to the intervention
◆ failing to communicate the intervention's lack of progress
◆ giving learners or stakeholders a false impression about their responsibilities in the intervention or the amount of effort required of them.

A fear of confrontation with the client or an unwillingness to admit that the time and resources needed to implement the intervention are underestimated may cause such ethical breaches. The consequences of these ethical breaches may be that the intervention fails, the WLP practitioner loses credibility, or the organization experiences various negative repercussions from the failed attempt.

Change Management

Possible ethical breaches that could occur in change management include:

- allowing the intervention to continue, despite the fact that it is causing an inappropriate level of trauma within the organization
- knowingly excluding appropriate individuals or groups in the change process
- not providing employees with the skills and tools they need to effectively adapt to the changes
- discontinuing communication with the organization because of controversy over the intervention.

Goal displacement may worsen these breaches. *Goal displacement* refers to a loss of focus on achieving the intended results. The cause of these breaches may include inexperience on the part of the WLP practitioner, fear of conflict, or bad planning of the intervention implementation. The consequences of these ethical breaches may include increased turnover rates, a rise in the number and severity of interpersonal conflicts, and a further loss of productivity within the organization.

Evaluation

During evaluation, WLP practitioners oversee the process of measuring results. Possible ethical breaches during this phase include:

- conducting evaluations based on data that is convenient and available rather than truly indicative of the intervention's impact
- intentionally developing an evaluation instrument that does not measure the desired outcomes of the intervention (for example, evaluating what facts participants learned in a training experience when the desired result was a change in on-the-job behavior)
- intentionally attributing changes in performance directly to a single intervention when a number of factors have contributed to the change
- ignoring evaluation results that do not match the original hypothesis of the analyst
- failing to admit that an intervention did not produce the desired effect.

A lack of expertise in applying methods, a failure to conduct a proper cause.analysis at the outset, a lack of awareness of the importance of evaluation, a lack of time and other resources, or a desire to make the intervention appear more successful than it really is may cause these breaches. The consequence is that the cli-

ent gets a false impression of the intervention's success and may assume that the problem is solved. The continuing existence of the problem may cause the client to lose additional time and productivity, may shatter employees' expectations for positive change, and may cause the WLP practitioner to lose all credibility.

If the WLP practitioner continually carries out these HPI activities in an ineffective and unethical manner, the loss of credibility can eventually extend beyond that practitioner. In fact, if ineffective WLP practitioners gain a reputation for spending their clients' money without producing the desired results, they may eventually harm the entire field of WLP. Already many stakeholders are suspicious of independent consultants who promise results that seem too good to be true. Practitioners in this field can avoid earning the negative stereotype attributed to used car salesmen by avoiding making false promises of unrealistic results.

Ethical Considerations Stemming From Trends Affecting WLP

Recall from section two the key trends affecting WLP:

1. Skill requirements will continue to increase in response to rapid technological change.
2. The American workforce will be significantly more educated and diverse.
3. Corporate restructuring will continue to reshape the business environment.
4. The size and composition of training departments will change dramatically.
5. Advances in technology will revolutionize training delivery.
6. Training departments will find new ways to deliver services.
7. There will be more focus on performance improvement.
8. Integrated high-performance work systems will proliferate.
9. Companies will transform into learning organizations.
10. Organizational emphasis on human performance management will accelerate (Bassi et al, 1997a).

Although these trends drive change, they also present a host of ethical dilemmas for the WLP practitioner. Each of these 10 trends falls into one of three categories: changes in the workforce, changes in organizational structure and culture, and changes in workplace learning strategies. These categories help to illustrate the relationship between ethics and trends. In some manner, changes in technology run throughout each of these categories. For this reason, one cannot consider changes in technology independently.

Changes in the Workforce (Trends One and Two)

In a recent survey conducted by ASTD, executive-level HRD managers reported "keeping pace with the rate of change" in technology as their number one challenge (1997 National HRD Executive Survey). In fact, this phenomenon is having a profound impact on the workforce (see trend one). Failing to balance technological change with humanistic considerations represents a large potential for ethical breaches in WLP. Although practitioners may easily quantify the monetary advantages of using technology to improve productivity, they may find it more difficult to quantify the monetary advantages of using learning interventions to increase the organization's intellectual capital. This does not mean that technological solutions are necessarily more effective than increased learning interventions. In addition, WLP practitioners cannot implement technological solutions in a vacuum. The introduction of new technologies in the workplace often necessitates new skills for the workforce. Line managers and WLP practitioners share an equal responsibility to update employee skills when they update technology. Unfortunately, technological solutions can consume vast amounts of financial and human resources, leaving very few resources for learning opportunities. On a nationwide scale, the amount of money that corporations spend on technology versus training exemplifies this phenomenon. In 1996, private corporations spent in excess of $500 billion on new technology, compared to $52 billion on training and development. Just the cost of fixing the "year 2000" problem in older computer programs is estimated to run $50 to $100 billion before the end of this millennium (*USA Today*, 1998). When confronted with the overwhelming costs of technology, organizations are understandably reluctant to dedicate precious resources to activities that cannot prove a direct correlation to increased profits. ASTD is working to remedy this problem by conducting research that correlates Kirkpatrick's Level I and Level III training evaluation data with stock performance. Until ASTD can substantiate that correlation, WLP practitioners must advocate for longer term solutions that raise the organization's intellectual capital. Technology and intellectual capital should not have to compete with each other for an organization's focus. The ultimate goal of everyone within the organization should be to achieve a balanced scorecard by integrating the benefits of technology and intellectual capital.

The following possible ethical breaches may be linked to trend one:

♦ ignoring or understating the costs and effort associated with upgrading the skills of employees who must cope with changing performance expectations resulting from the introduction of new technology
♦ advocating for a pure technological solution without considering its impact on the workforce
♦ terminating underskilled employees in lieu of providing sufficient learning opportunities and time for them to adapt to changing skill requirements
♦ knowingly ignoring the learning requirements, social needs, and human-related factors associated with technological change.

Ethical considerations may also arise from an American workforce that will grow significantly more educated and diverse (trend two). Organizations have an obligation to establish and maintain an environment that supports a diverse workforce. They must do more than create a set of policies for dealing with diversity issues and strictly enforce them. Although these steps may lead to a reduction in flagrant violations of civil liberties, they do not begin to address how the organization can use its diverse workforce for generating innovative products that have a wide appeal to the global population. Organizations also need to find new ways to incorporate the knowledge and experience of highly educated employees who can greatly increase the amount of innovation that takes place within the organization. Here again, simply having policies and procedures that entitle employees to power is only a superficial attempt to tap into these vast human resources. True empowerment must encompass an entire system of support that includes coaching, mentoring, rewards, equipment, and access to information resources.

The following possible ethical breaches may be linked to trend two:

♦ recommending interventions that make sweeping changes in corporate culture, without fully understanding the impact these changes will produce
♦ knowingly using interventions that ignore the special needs, talents, or abilities of individuals
♦ making individual employment decisions based on factors other than the prospective employee's ability to achieve desired performance results or to learn the work
♦ limiting an employee's access to information in order to hide unethical practices of the organization.

Changes in Organizational Structure and Culture (Trends Three, Eight, Nine, and 10)

The 1990s will probably go down in the history of business as the era of corporate restructuring. A recent survey by the Bureau of Labor Statistics found that restructuring efforts have affected 57 percent of all white-collar American workers. Corporate restructuring efforts have drastically reshaped the business environment and have presented a host of ethical issues for the WLP profession (trend three).

Some evidence suggests that corporations sometimes undertake restructuring without due consideration for the long-term impact on the organization's performance, profitability, or competitiveness (Cascio, 1993; Church, 1998). In such situations, organizations may terminate experienced employees who embody knowledge capital in order to reap short-term savings. Organizations are often amazingly nearsighted when they announce a major reorganization effort. Although the intent is to become leaner and meaner, the result is often disappointing. In times of great uncertainty, the first people to secure employment elsewhere are usually the most skilled, educated, and productive employees who work for the organization. This means that, although the organization may find it less painful and difficult to reach their new workforce numbers, maintaining the same level of skilled employees proves quite difficult. In effect, the result is a depleted pool of talented employees, and competitors gain valuable intellectual assets (Pace University, 1998). A recent study of organizations that have either merged or downsized in the 1990s found that only 17 percent have demonstrated substantial returns in shareholder equity (MC Associates, 1996). WLP practitioners can be instrumental in helping organizations understand and deal with this phenomenon.

The following possible ethical breaches may be linked to trend three:

◆ accepting cost reduction as the "right" solution without considering revenue enhancement or productivity improvement alternatives
◆ knowingly accepting short-term solutions that have a high probability of creating performance problems with immediate and long-term impact
◆ not taking the risk to explain the full implications of corporate restructuring in order to preserve a personal relationship with the organization.

Ethical breaches may also result from the proliferation of integrated high-performance work systems (trend eight) and from an increased focus on performance improvement (trend 10). WLP practitioners will be under increasing pressure to define, implement, and evaluate effective human performance management systems. Doing so will require an intimate understanding of business processes, business drivers, business problems, and the potential benefits of aligning the organization's resources. WLP practitioners will help organizations to establish performance targets, determine performance gaps, discover the root causes for performance gaps, integrate the processes of various departments, increase communication between groups, and hold employees accountable for reaching the organization's goals. At the same time, however, practitioners will need to strike a difficult balance between business needs and humanistic considerations.

◆ ◆ ◆

Corporate restructuring efforts have drastically reshaped the business environment and have presented a host of ethical issues for the WLP profession.

◆ ◆ ◆

To build high-performance work teams, one must consider humanistic needs and organizational needs simultaneously. To improve its productivity, an organization must address interpersonal barriers while also examining the organization's processes, information systems, and rewards programs. Furthermore, all of these activities must focus on achieving business results (for example, raising sales figures, lowering the amount of turnover, and lowering the amount of rework). If practitioners fail to direct their interventions toward solving business needs, stakeholders will not find great value in their efforts. For example, if a WLP practitioner manages to raise the average scores on an employee satisfaction survey, without ascertaining the financial effect of this increased morale, the stakeholders may cease to find value in this endeavor. Therefore, integrating work teams is not enough if the teams' results are not quantifiable in the language of business results. The following are possible ethical breaches that may occur when one tries to establish and maintain this balance:

◆ Overemphasis on humanistic or organizational needs at the expense of the other.
◆ The intentional misrepresentation to stakeholders that performance can be improved without due consideration of organizational or humanistic needs.

- Attempts to apply a solution that is familiar to the WLP practitioner but is not appropriate to the situation at hand.
- Honoring of a client's request to institute teams in inappropriate situations. Line managers who do not fully understand the true requirements for supporting a team-based structure often prompt requests for teams. In these situations, the manager is simply trying to boost productivity by renaming the "department" a "team." This misunderstanding will probably lead to a botched attempt at teamwork.

Ethical issues may arise when traditional organizations try to transform themselves into learning organizations (see trend nine). If organizations attempt this transition without a complete understanding of what learning organizations are, they are highly likely to be disappointed. WLP practitioners may find that managers are uncertain of how to establish and maintain learning organizations and of how they lead to increased productivity.

The following examples of possible ethical breaches may be linked to trend nine:

- applying generic and potentially ineffective practices for expedience or ease rather than defining the learning organization in the context of one corporate culture with unique decision makers, customers, and stakeholders
- creating the expectation that WLP practitioners can generate conditions characterizing a learning organization quickly, without much work, or with limited resources
- "selling" the idea of learning organizations to stakeholders as a cure-all for performance problems.

Changes in Workplace Learning Strategies (Trends Four, Five, Six, and Seven)

As the size and composition of training departments dramatically change (trend four), several ethical considerations may arise. As trainers are required to do far more with far less, they will experience considerable work-related stress. They will have to satisfy increasingly sophisticated and discriminating stakeholders who include top managers, line managers, other employees, and the organization's customers. They may have difficulty securing the resources they need for assisting in a wide array of performance improvement initiatives. This situation will tempt WLP practitioners to cut corners in order to survive in this environment. Rather than struggling to survive, WLP practitioners will need to step back and take a strategic look at the services they provide. In many circumstances, they may

need to outsource certain services or to offer fewer, higher quality products. Also, some of the strategies outlined in trends five and six will assist the new training organization in establishing these new processes.

The following examples of possible ethical breaches may be linked to trend four:

- knowingly recommending or implementing training interventions not linked to organizational strategic objectives or to customers' needs
- knowingly accepting WLP efforts without establishing learner and stakeholder accountability or without allotting sufficient time or resources.

An increased reliance on learning technologies and other alternative forms of distributing information to learners (trends five and six) will also present a host of new ethical dilemmas for trainers and other WLP professionals. The driving force behind both of these trends is an organization's desire to lower training costs, increase accessibility to learning programs, diminish a learner's time spent away from the job, and provide training within the workplace setting. Organizations will accomplish these goals through the use of technological applications and alternative forms of training delivery such as coaching, line manager facilitation, self-study courses, performance support tools, and various types of job aids. Regardless of the strategy, WLP practitioners must be vigilant in determining if these alternative forms of learning are capable of truly imparting new skills and knowledge. Simply agreeing to these strategies in order to appear current with modern notions of learning may spell disaster for the WLP practitioner. At the same time, WLP practitioners will need to apply this same level of scrutiny to information delivered via traditional classroom training.

Although in many cases technology may be an appropriate means of distributing training to an audience separated in time and place, in other cases the implementation of learning technologies may be the result of a misguided decision. An example of this misguided decision is a trainer's introduction of learning technologies simply in response to an executive's edict to deliver training via the company's new intranet. If a trainer blindly follows this edict, without considering the types of information contained in the programs or the needs of the learners, the end result is likely to disappoint. Many stakeholders do not fully understand the range of costs and time constraints imposed by technological solutions.

The following possible ethical breaches may be linked to trends five and six:

- knowingly recommending or adopting unnecessary technologies (known as technolust)
- intentionally failing to consider the full costs, time requirements, and importance of learner involvement in applying technology-based delivery methods
- selecting technologies that offer an easier implementation process for the WLP practitioner or a reduced cost for the organization, at the expense of the learners
- not equipping line managers with the tools they need to perform on-the-job training and coaching, in order to make formal training appear more effective
- not remaining objective about the effectiveness of alternative forms of training delivery due to a bias toward classroom training.

Other ethical breaches may result from an increased focus on performance improvement (trend seven). Many people in the HRD field are concerned that an exclusive emphasis on HPI may lead to dehumanizing activities that elevate productivity but create work environments that are not people friendly and ethically oriented. Although HPI does take a more scientific approach toward analyzing and solving gaps in performance, it should never assert organizational needs at the expense of the employees. Although many performance improvement strategies will cause a certain degree of trauma to the people within the organization, the WLP practitioner should work to keep the trauma at a reasonable level. In many cases, the cure is worse than the problem, and therefore the intervention is not justifiable. This consideration is both humanistic and economic. An organization cannot function properly and be profitable if its employees feel assaulted by change initiatives. Furthermore, the WLP practitioner bears a responsibility to monitor the changes that are occurring and to help the workforce to adapt to those changes in the best possible way.

The following possible ethical breaches may be linked to trend seven:

- allowing short-term cost reductions or productivity increases to take precedence over long-term customer or employee satisfaction
- viewing performance improvement as the only goal—without regard to balancing individual and organizational needs or considering ethical issues
- allowing performance improvement interventions to continue, although the level of trauma they are causing to employees is overwhelming

- replacing incumbent workers with new workers in order to avoid training and development costs—incumbent workers deserve a chance to develop the skills necessary to accomplish the desired level of performance.

Avoiding Ethical Breaches

Although outlining ethical breaches is important, one also must provide strategies for avoiding them. The basis for avoiding ethical breaches is to consider each intervention strategy carefully before implementing it. The age-old practice of questioning is the most effective way of considering the effects of an implementation. In fact, asking the right questions at the appropriate times is more critical to success in this field than knowing all of the correct answers. Five questions present the critical issues that one should consider when weighing the advantages and disadvantages of various solutions. Each can be useful in helping WLP practitioners avoid ethical breaches.

- Question 1: *What is just and fair?* The goal is to seek equality through some set of subjective measures. Perceptions of justice are subject to current cultural views and norms. The majority of people within the organization or society affected by the decision should agree with these views and norms. By carefully considering these questions, WLP practitioners can increase the chances that employees will view the decision positively and incorporate it into their daily work practices.
- Question 2: *What leads to moderation?* The goal is to avoid extremes and to seek balance. As described by Aristotle, the truth usually lies somewhere in the "middle path." Although finding this middle path is not easy, examining the extremes is a worthwhile pursuit because it helps practitioners to understand the underlying assumptions that exist at the extreme views. They face less risk of ethical breaches by operating in a balanced environment.
- Question 3: *What results does an action or behavior seek?* The goal is to analyze desired results. Given the emphasis of WLP on results, this strategy is often preferred, however, the practitioner also must determine if the desired results are ethical. For instance, if increased profitability is a desired result, the organization should not achieve it at the expense of basic humanistic concerns such as fair wages and safe tools.
- Question 4: *What works best over the long term?* The WLP practitioner must determine which options hold the best chance of being sustainable over the

long term and which options best balance organizational and humanistic needs. The general public is most likely to consider options that meet both sets of criteria as ethical.

◆ Question 5: *How would you like to be treated under the same circumstances?* A fifth and final way to avoid a breach of ethics is to apply the golden rule, Do unto others as you would have them do unto you. The answer to the question should provide guidance for avoiding an ethical breach. Although this approach may sound simplistic, it can force a WLP practitioner to take a look at the underlying issues creating the ethical dilemma.

Section Summary

This section defined *ethics* as principles about right and wrong and good and bad. *Ethics* also refers to a system of moral principles, values, rules or standards governing a profession, occupation, or industry.

Ethics are important to WLP practitioners for several reasons. One reason is that they face many ethical challenges in their work. A second reason is that WLP practitioners are often responsible for helping organizations establish their codes of ethics and for designing and delivering training on ethics. A third reason is that an organization's reputation—a function of how it engages in business practice and thereby maintains the trust of customers and employees—is key to effective performance and customer service.

Ethical considerations in WLP may stem from applying steps in the WLP process model and from the trends affecting WLP. This section listed possible ethical breaches linked to the steps in the HPI process of performance analysis, cause analysis, intervention selection, intervention implementation, change management, and evaluation. This section also listed possible ethical considerations stemming from trends affecting WLP.

Finally, this section suggested that those who bear responsibility for WLP should ask five questions when confronted with ethical dilemmas. These questions may serve to shed light on what decision is ethical and moral in a specific situation.

This section suggests ways to apply the model, roles, competencies, outputs, future trends, and ethical issues presented in this book in different organizational settings. ASTD's members and WLP practitioners work in a variety of organizational settings including government agencies (state, local, and federal), military establishments, nonprofit organizations, corporations, and academic institutions. This volume can be useful to practitioners in a broad array of organizational settings, but some of the role, competency, and output descriptions may require further detail before readers can apply them to unique circumstances and needs. In particular, demonstrating how this information applies to true bottom-line issues such as return-on-investment is extremely important. The reader must remember to embellish on the competencies, roles, and outputs so that this link to bottom-line issues will be clear and so that the book's language will match the language of the individual organization. This adjustment should not be difficult because the way these roles, competencies, and outputs function does not differ much from organization to organization.

Uses for Practitioners

This volume describes the competencies that individuals charged with WLP responsibilities should possess. Of course, individuals bearing WLP responsibilities will perform many roles, possess many competencies, and produce many work outputs. The range of what they do and what stakeholders will expect of them will vary dramatically from organization to organization. WLP professionals may function as generalists or specialists. Generalists perform most of the roles described in this study, whereas specialists focus on a limited number of roles. This book will serve as a valuable resource for anyone charged with responsibility for WLP.

Identifying or Clarifying Work Expectations and Competency Levels

This volume provides a useful starting point for identifying what competencies WLP professionals should possess now and in five years. Readers can use the HPI process model and the lists of roles, competencies, and sample outputs as starting points for identifying the tools they require now and will require in five years. They can also use these tools as a reference to begin a discussion with stakeholders and clarify stakeholder expectations.

Designing Jobs, Work, or Tasks

This book is a valuable tool for helping individuals design their jobs and work tasks. It is an excellent guide

for recruiting or orienting WLP practitioners because it provides a menu of possible roles and associated competencies. Similarly, senior managers and other stakeholders can use this book for establishing expectations for individuals charged with WLP responsibilities.

Managing Projects

The HPI process model is a flexible blueprint for organizing WLP projects that are intended to improve human performance and encourage individual, group, or organizational learning. The WLP roles, competencies, sample outputs, and HPI process model can become a basis for planning and monitoring WLP projects.

Prompting Feedback on Performance

Improved feedback can prompt development and learning. This principle applies as much to WLP work as it does to all other kinds of work. By using the roles, competencies, and outputs described in this book, WLP professionals can solicit meaningful feedback about their performance from their customers. This feedback can improve a WLP professional's performance and increase his or her career development.

Planning for Careers

Jobs within HRD have traditionally fallen within one of three disciplines: training and development, organization development, and career development. Because WLP professionals will undertake a broader array of functions, they must begin preparing themselves for careers in many disciplines. The ability to cultivate organizational learning and to improve human performance have become key skills for leaders throughout organizations. The key to a successful WLP career in the future will be aligning WLP skills with the needs of organizational leaders and line managers. This study has begun to establish a framework around which to build such an alignment. WLP professionals will take one of the first steps in establishing this alignment by rapidly increasing their knowledge of learning technology. Such knowledge will help the WLP professional to build credibility with organizational leaders and will provide a basis for future relationships with line managers.

Identifying Professional Development Needs

This volume can help individuals responsible for WLP to examine their professional development needs and to identify areas in which they may need to increase their knowledge. Readers can use the set of competency assessment tools for benchmarking. They also can use the assessment results to create personal development plans.

Documenting Accomplishments

This volume provides the basis for developing a common language across organizations. By documenting work accomplishments in terms of the roles, competencies, and outputs described in this book, individuals can substantiate the tools they have acquired in their unique corporate cultures. This documentation is valuable to WLP practitioners because it is transferable between organizations or between departments. It is particularly valuable to individuals making changes in their careers.

◆ ◆ ◆

Gone are the days when HRD professionals were solely responsible for employee development. WLP practitioners today help employees identify their individual learning needs and then steer them toward the resources they need for effective self-development.

◆ ◆ ◆

Training Others

Gone are the days when HRD professionals were solely responsible for employee development. WLP practitioners today help employees identify their individual learning needs and then steer them toward the resources they need for effective self-development. This development will usually include a mix of formal learning events (for example, training) and informal learning opportunities (for example, surfing the Web for information). This volume is a starting point for structuring an organizational learning program, and it serves many groups inside and outside organizations including employees, managers, and customers.

Consulting With Others

This book provides a springboard for traditional trainers or HRD practitioners to become WLP practitioners. The HPI process model provides a useful and flexible blueprint to guide consulting engagements, whether carried out by internal or external WLP practitioners.

Preparing for the Future

Those who perform WLP work can prepare themselves for the future by referring to the 10 trends identified in this volume. Clearly, the WLP field is heading toward an increased emphasis on achieving business results (that is, improved performance) and a decreased emphasis on orchestrating activities such as training. By considering how trends are affecting the WLP field,

practitioners can formulate strategies to solve organizational problems, boost intellectual capital, and prepare the organization for the future.

Maintaining Ethical Standards

Ethics scandals wrack business, government, and nonprofit organizations, and WLP practitioners often bear an important responsibility for maintaining and perpetuating ethical standards. Those performing WLP work can use the list of ethical issues supplied in section six to

◆ identify ethical issues of greatest importance in their current work
◆ identify ways of responding to those issues
◆ help their organizations establish codes of ethics and codes of conduct
◆ help their organizations maintain a climate conducive to ethical practices.

Uses for WLP Managers

A WLP manager is anyone bearing key responsibility for oversight and facilitation of WLP work (with or without a staff). WLP managers will find this book useful for helping them meet their responsibilities.

Reinventing the Role of the Training Department

Many organizations are reengineering their training departments by placing emphasis on HPI. They may, however, begin to rely too heavily on short-term management interventions such as rewards and recognition programs. This overreliance may harm the long-term viability of the organization. The training professionals should reposition themselves strategically so that they can work toward HPI and place appropriate emphasis on developing intellectual capital.

This book offers a vision of what a reinvented training department should look like and what reinvented trainers should focus on. It can help facilitate a training department's transition into a WLP department.

Staff Planning

This volume provides valuable information on what types of skills and knowledge WLP practitioners need. It also provides a starting point for

◆ assessing the competency levels of existing staff
◆ managing outsourcing opportunities
◆ hiring vendors and consultants
◆ identifying or clarifying work expectations of those performing WLP work or others playing a role in establishing and implementing WLP strategy

- designing jobs and work tasks for those performing WLP work
- overseeing WLP projects
- providing feedback on performance to those doing WLP work
- offering advice and consultation about career planning to those performing WLP work
- identifying the professional development needs of those performing WLP work
- documenting the accomplishments of those who perform WLP work
- teaching employees about short-term, intermediate-term, and long-term efforts intended to improve human performance through individual, group, or organizational learning.

Preparing for the Future

WLP managers bear responsibility for helping their organizations set their future directions. This responsibility is complicated by dynamic trends that change an organization's internal and external environment. The future trends identified in this book help the reader to begin thinking about ways that WLP should position itself to anticipate the impact of those trends.

Maintaining Ethical Standards

WLP managers should establish a climate in which those who perform WLP work can carry out their roles, demonstrate their competencies, and produce outputs in a high-performance, high-involvement, and learning-supportive environment. This book provides a tool for examining ethical issues and crafting codes of ethics for those performing WLP work. These codes will help the WLP manager to hold individuals accountable for ethical standards and solve ethical dilemmas as they arise.

Establishing Clear Expectations and Accountabilities

A unique feature of this study is that it examines the importance of future competencies for WLP work from three perspectives: (1) practitioners; (2) selected senior

◆ ◆ ◆

WLP managers should establish a climate in which those who perform WLP work can carry out their roles, demonstrate their competencies, and produce outputs in a high-performance, high-involvement, and learning-supportive environment.

◆ ◆ ◆

practitioners; and (3) line managers. This three-phase analysis compares and contrasts the perceptions of each of these groups, including the perspective of WLP customers (that is, line managers). Understanding the line manager's perspective should help WLP practitioners to promote the study's findings to their own management-level stakeholders and to receive a greater level of buy-in from their customers.

Uses for Line Managers

A line manager is anyone bearing primary responsibility for serving customers, making products, dealing with suppliers, and meeting the needs of distributors. In most organizations the majority of employees report to line managers. In manufacturing firms, line managers focus on the manufacturing process, and in service firms line managers focus on service delivery. Line managers are distinct from staff managers, who provide expert advice in a special area and support line managers in their work.

Finding New Ways to Increase Employee Knowledge

Line managers bear primary responsibility for fostering human learning in their departments. Line managers have two categories of learning techniques at their disposal: formal and informal learning. Formal learning often involves a specific event that occurs outside the workplace setting. Training and college courses are the most obvious examples. Informal learning can include individual coaching, group coaching, mentoring, accessing new information, and using job aids. Depending on the manner of its implementation, on-the-job training can be either formal or informal. For example, a line manager who spends the entire day demonstrating how to operate a particular machine would be giving formal training (even though it technically may occur in a workplace setting). However, a line manager who gives employees a manual and tells them to figure out how to operate the machine and produce as many widgets as they can would be providing informal training. Line managers must look continuously for innovative ways to increase the intellectual capital of their staff members. If they solely rely on a traditional training department to impart new skills and knowledge, they will always find their employees falling behind in necessary learning. Professional instructional designers need a great deal of time to diagnose the training need, understand the desired process, create the course, train employees, and evaluate the results. Although this process is vital for some learning efforts, the line manager can scale back the process when the new skills are just extensions of existing skills.

Finding New Ways to Increase Employee Performance

Line managers also must play a pivotal role in determining human performance gaps, uncovering the root causes for these gaps, selecting appropriate improvement strategies, implementing these strategies, managing the change process, and evaluating performance. Without a deep commitment from line managers, WLP practitioners cannot use the HPI process to enact meaningful changes. This book provides a common ground and a common language for line managers and WLP practitioners to use when creating meaningful strategies for their organizations.

Evaluating and Measuring Results

Section four describes a process for determining culturally specific outputs affecting WLP competencies. This process can help line managers determine what deliverables their staff—and WLP professionals—should be producing and assist them in evaluating the quality of those deliverables.

Uses for Employees

Just as *ASTD Models for Human Performance Improvement* (Rothwell, 1996a) advocates for employee involvement in HPI efforts, this book advocates for employee participation in improving performance and in building intellectual capital. Along with greater employee involvement in organizational strategies comes an expectation of employee responsibility for learning and increasing the organization's intellectual capital. Furthermore, all employees must be responsible for establishing a work environment conducive to high performance.

Interacting Effectively With the Training, WLP, or HPI Department

The processes, roles, and methodology for determining outputs described in this book can help employees understand the WLP function and determine how this function will best serve them in their work responsibilities. Employees need to understand that WLP is not the product of one person or one department. It involves everyone in the organization, and professional WLP practitioners must work hand in hand with line managers and employees to produce meaningful results. A large part of WLP success will depend on a change in employees' perceptions. Employees must understand that WLP is not just a new name for training and that they share in the responsibility for learning and improving performance.

Analyzing Performance Gaps and Determining Their Causes

Employees bear responsibility for helping managers and WLP practitioners pinpoint performance improvement opportunities. This book provides a starting point for training employees who need to identify occasions when HPI strategies are necessary, appropriate, and desirable.

Choosing and Implementing WLP Strategies

Employees play a major part in choosing and implementing WLP strategies. This book will be useful to those who teach employees about their roles in formulating and implementing WLP strategies that can dramatically increase the organization's intellectual capital and overall performance.

Uses for Academicians

A number of undergraduate and graduate programs in training and development and HRD exist around the world. Administrators, faculty, and staff working in these programs will find this book useful for many purposes.

Assessing Needs

This volume provides a framework for conducting academic program needs assessments that

◆ assess the demand of employers for graduates who are able to apply the principles of WLP
◆ assess interest in academic coursework in WLP among prospective students.

Planning Programs and Courses

The WLP roles and competencies described in this book provide a basis for

◆ establishing new courses or revising old courses based on WLP roles, competencies, trends, and ethical issues
◆ benchmarking this study against programs offered at academic institutions.

Assessing Learners

This volume provides a framework for

◆ measuring the capabilities of prospective or current students against the competencies listed in this study
◆ assessing the differences between individual student competencies and the competencies required for present and future success in WLP.

◆ ◆ ◆

Accountability *is the key word for the 1990s.*

◆ ◆ ◆

Formulating and Implementing a Research Agenda

This study does not claim to answer all relevant questions about the field of WLP. In fact, it is only the beginning of a research agenda (that is, a long-range plan to guide research) that will need to answer many more questions about the WLP field. Future studies must address questions such as the following:

◆ How do the roles, competencies, outputs, ethical issues, and trends identified in this study match up to the expectations of chief executive officers, senior executives, middle managers, and customers?
◆ What similarities and differences may exist between applications of WLP in the United States and in other nations or cultures?
◆ How do emerging technologies affect the roles, competencies, and outputs of WLP work?

Advising Learners

Students enrolled in academic programs often need advice on what courses to take, what career goals to pursue, and how to build the competencies they will need to realize their career goals. This book is a useful tool for organizing such discussions. By using the lists of competencies and roles provided, faculty and students can ensure that they address the major components of WLP work.

Managing and Developing Faculty

Faculty members who teach in WLP academic programs must stay current with changes in the business world if they are to teach effectively and provide appropriate guidance to students. This book provides a useful framework for assessing faculty competencies and suggesting professional development opportunities.

Evaluating Program Processes and Results

Accountability is the key word for the 1990s. Just as WLP practitioners are under mounting pressure to demonstrate their effectiveness, academic programs are also under mounting pressure to demonstrate that they are delivering effective instruction. This book is a standard against which to evaluate academic programs and ensure their close alignment to the needs of work organizations such as businesses, agencies, and nonprofit enterprises. External review teams that evaluate academic programs may rely on this book as a benchmark for assessing an academic WLP program.

Section Summary

Anyone charged with WLP responsibilities may apply the information contained in this book. This section offered suggestions for WLP practitioners, WLP managers, line managers, employees, and academicians about the many ways they may apply the findings presented in this book. Table 7.1 provides a summary of these uses.

Table 7.1: Uses for *ASTD Models for Workplace Learning and Performance*

Audience	Possible Uses
• WLP practitioners	• Preparation for entry into WLP work • Preparation for assumption of more responsibility in WLP or broader responsibility for WLP work • Design or organization of work tasks • Career planning • Personal or professional development • Recording of personal or professional accomplishments
• WLP managers	• Introduction of line managers and top managers to WLP—and to their roles in building, sustaining, and increasing the impact of intellectual capital • Linking of WLP to the organization's strategic plan, objectives, and competitive approaches • Educating line managers and top managers about possible expanded roles for WLP professionals in the organization • Reexamination of the mission of the WLP function • Reexamination of staffing requirements of the WLP function • Assessment and development of WLP staff members • Establishment of the basis for an organization-specific code of ethics for those performing WLP work • Offering career advice and guidance to WLP staff members and others
• Line managers	• Education about their possible roles in performing WLP work • Education about contributions that WLP can make to the organization and to the line managers' areas of responsibility • Preparation for coaching their full-time and part-time employees to take more active roles in learning and development as they perform their work
• Employees and learners	• Education about their possible roles in WLP • Education about the contributions that WLP can make to the organization and to the employees' or learners' areas of responsibility • Preparation for coaching colleagues to take more active roles in their own learning and development with the goal of improved performance in mind
• Academics	• Conducting of needs assessment for academic programs in WLP or related fields • Conducting of academic program reviews • Establishment of academic program curricula • Development of course curricula • Establishment of a research agenda • Advising of students • Personal and professional development • Application of WLP principles to academic institutions

SECTION 1	BACKGROUND

SECTION 2	TRENDS

SECTION 3	THE STUDY

SECTION 4	ROLES, COMPETENCIES, AND OUTPUTS

SECTION 5	RESULTS OF THE STUDY

SECTION 6	ETHICAL CHALLENGES

SECTION 7	SUGGESTED AUDIENCES AND USES

SECTION 8	CONCLUSION

- ◆ The Continual Evolution of Roles and Competencies
- ◆ The Essential Basics
- ◆ Learning Technologies: A Bridge to the Future
- ◆ The Need to Align Line Manager and Practitioner Expectations for WLP Service
- ◆ WLP Teamwork
- ◆ Leadership: A Two-Way Street
- ◆ The Increasing Importance of Intellectual Capital
- ◆ The Human Side of the Equation
- ◆ The Global Future

Previous sections presented much information about the similarities and differences between the three respondent groups. This section will focus on pulling all of this information together into a cohesive understanding. The recommendations discussed are based on the data but also contain elements of the researchers' and authors' experiences in the field. Although these recommendations may not apply to every reader's situation, they should provide a general road map of how one can become more engaged in the WLP field and develop his or her proficiencies in the required skills.

The Continual Evolution of Roles and Competencies

One of the greatest dangers in publishing a competency study is that readers could get the false impression that the competencies and roles established in the study will be always applicable to the profession. At best, this is wishful thinking. At worst, this impression will lead readers into a false sense of security about their careers. The reality is that competencies and roles are moving targets. Not only do they vary tremendously by discipline, industry, and organization, but changes in the general marketplace will inevitably change the competencies and roles needed to meet this new reality. Consideration of these facts may raise the question, "Why study competencies and roles?" The answer is that WLP practitioners need to know where they have been in order to know where they are going. Although this study is future oriented, it cannot guarantee that the competencies needed for success in five years will indeed be the 52 competencies presented in this book. Though potentially overwhelming, this concept is important to grasp. Certainly these competencies can help readers to align themselves with an organization's current and future needs, but readers must maintain a critical eye when examining the changing world around them.

Roles, competencies, and outputs evolve over time: they do not remain static. Changes in WLP roles, competencies, and outputs are a function of changes in (1) the external environment, (2) the clients or customers who depend on the outcomes of the work, (3) the people who perform the work, and (4) the work itself.

First, trends in the external environment create pressure for organizational responses. WLP practitioners cannot enact the same roles, demonstrate the same competencies, or produce the same outputs forever when facing demands to help their organizations grapple with the challenges wrought by such trends as the continuous introduction of new technology, the pervasive influence of globalization, or the pressures created by continuing efforts to contain costs and increase pro-

ductivity. Meeting these challenges requires new approaches; and these new approaches, in turn, require that WLP practitioners respond with new roles, demonstrate new competencies, and produce new outputs.

Second, as client or customer demands change in response to trends and organizational challenges, people in traditional roles in any field must adjust or risk customer dissatisfaction. For the many customers of WLP—including line managers, workers, suppliers, distributors, prospective workers, and government regulators—as demands on them change, their expectations of people in WLP roles change. Hence, WLP practitioners face changes in role expectations as their customers encounter new workplace learning demands and grapple with new workplace performance challenges.

◆ ◆ ◆

Changes in WLP roles, competencies, and outputs are a function of changes in (1) the external environment, (2) the clients or customers who depend on the outcomes of the work, (3) the people who perform the work, and (4) the work itself.

◆ ◆ ◆

Third, the individuals who carry out WLP are also changing. More individuals with professional preparation are entering the WLP field. This change is the result of a burgeoning number of increasingly sophisticated undergraduate, graduate, and certificate programs in the field. As individuals graduate from these programs and demonstrate what they can do in the workplace, they change what others expect of them—and change the roles, competencies, and outputs typical to the WLP field.

Fourth and finally, the work of WLP itself is changing. Not too long ago, many people closely associated training with classroom-based instruction. But now, increasingly, many people associate WLP with technology-based initiatives capable of reaching many people over great distances and across time zones. Working with learning technologies creates new demands on trainers and other WLP practitioners. As a consequence, their roles, competencies, and expected work outputs change accordingly.

The Essential Basics

Traditional HRD activities such as competency identification, communication, and standards identification are still important to line managers. Although this competency study suggests new ways that WLP practitioners can add value to their organizations, they should not neglect their traditional core competencies. An interesting debate takes place in many training departments about whether it is proper to supply a service to a customer when the trainer knows that training will not fix the problem and has communicated this to the customer, but the customer wants the training anyway. Perhaps the most common example of this is a line manager asking for stress management training when the trainers understand that the line manager is the "stressor." Convincing arguments support both sides of this debate, but the point is that WLP practitioners need to win credibility in order to secure future assignments that will make a difference in the organization. WLP practitioners need to build on their basic competencies so that they will be in a position to play a larger role in their organization's future decisions.

Learning Technologies: A Bridge to the Future

Although WLP professionals have many concerns about the effectiveness and ethics of teaching via electronic means, line managers definitely see a great potential for learning technologies. Line managers' hope that learning technologies will reduce training costs and decrease training time presents a magnificent opportunity for WLP professionals. The key is for these professionals to use electronic devices to further the learning experience, not just to lower training costs. Learning technologies represent the beginning of a learning revolution: The golden age of learning lies ahead. Learning technologies allow the tailoring of learning experiences to the individual and provide a medium that can use the Socratic method of teaching. Classroom instructors are lucky if they can find a way to cater to two or three learning styles simultaneously, whereas instruction designed for the desktop can cater to any learning style. In no way should this suggest that classroom training is going away. Classroom training will always provide an important environment for certain types of learning. Learning technologies simply provide another means for increasing learning.

The Need to Align Line Managers' and Practitioners' Expectations for WLP Service

Learning to see people as vital resources is a major mind shift for some line managers, and learning to focus on business results is a major mind shift for some HRD professionals. It is pointless to debate which

group requires the most education to understand how these two elements must come together for the good of the organization and the good of the employees. What is important to understand is that only through a balance of these elements can meaningful progress take place within an organization. Everyone should realize that, without people, a business is nothing, and without business results, people may lose their jobs.

Respondents repeatedly identified the "ability to see the 'big picture'" as important to success in the field and in business. In order to help lead organizations, WLP practitioners first must learn to see outside the traditional HRD box and grow to understand what makes an organization tick. Appendix A gives paraphrased quotes from the line managers' and WLP experts' original survey responses received during the data collection phase of this study. These quotes are a great place to start learning about the expectations and needs of these groups. Also, table 5.8 in section 5 demonstrates that WLP professionals must begin to show their ability to use analytical and business competencies if they are to take on a leadership role within organizations. If WLP professionals do not market themselves as strategic business partners, organizations will continue to view them as an expense rather than an investment.

◆ ◆ ◆

A WLP practitioner may be able to make an initial diagnosis concerning a performance problem, but representatives from many different parts of the organization will need to uncover the root causes and help to fix the problem.

◆ ◆ ◆

WLP Teamwork

Rating 52 current and future competencies against each other is an entirely different matter than trying to acquire all of these competencies. No individual, and perhaps no single department, will possess all of this knowledge. The very nature of WLP is an extremely complex phenomenon. Effectively carrying out WLP endeavors will require the combined efforts of many employees, from many departments and at many levels of the organization. Viewing the organization as an organism aids in these endeavors. Many different systems seem to be working independently of each other, but on closer inspection, every system depends on another. Consider an analogy with the various systems that make up a human organism. The digestive system, the cardiopulmonary system, the neurological system, and the reproductive system could not exist without each other. The various systems within an organization are similarly interdependent. A general practitioner in medicine makes an initial diagnosis and then consults with specialists to help solve the problem. A WLP practitioner may be able to make an initial diagnosis concerning a performance problem, but representatives from many different parts of the organization will need to uncover the root causes and help to fix the problem. WLP practitioners must not fool themselves into thinking that they can carry out WLP endeavors single-handedly.

Leadership: A Two-Way Street

Traditionally, HRD practitioners have provided leadership development for the top managers of the organization. In recent years, however, the idea has emerged that HRD practitioners themselves need to be organizational leaders. This idea does not suggest a corporate mutiny but an increased attempt to work with upper management in order to get them to understand the advantages that WLP holds for the organization. Several of the line managers who responded to the survey mentioned the need for WLP professionals to "educate senior management about best practices in human resources." Although today's WLP practitioners may hesitate to think of going over someone's head to get to the root causes of a problem, doing so may be essential. WLP practitioners do not need to become corporate rebels to cause positive change, but they do need to stand by their principles, be tenacious, and creatively find ways to influence the decision makers in their organizations. Human performance theory is not mysterious: When applied correctly and monitored carefully, it will produce the results that organizations seek. WLP practitioners must take leadership roles in their organizations to put these theories into practice.

The Increasing Importance of Intellectual Capital

Whether termed *knowledge management, intellectual capital, intellectual assets,* or *knowledge capital,* the idea that organizations must somehow capture, store, and disseminate the know-how that their employees produce is becoming vital to sustained competitiveness. As cyberspace blurs the international borders, determining where an organization's intellectual assets reside is becoming increasingly difficult. Fifteen years ago, most companies had a finite number of places where their employees worked. Today's employees are working everywhere—not only do they telecommute from their

homes, but they conduct business on planes, trains, cars, and even on the ski slope. The sheer portability of knowledge and information makes organizations vulnerable to the loss of intellectual assets. Certain legal steps can prevent the transfer of organizational knowledge, but documents such as noncompete clauses between an individual and an organization can rarely hold up in court. In general, the law does not allow an organization to prevent an individual from making a living. The same information that organizations want to keep proprietary is the lifeblood of an information age worker's career. Because organizations cannot "extract" knowledge from an employee who leaves an organization, they must find ways to leverage this knowledge as quickly as possible to use it to their competitive advantage. Organizations that are the quickest to use their new ideas tend to be the most successful.

Organizations today also are starting to use electronic support systems to help their employees get the information they need when they need it. These systems often require input from experts in order to function properly. This input, in turn, becomes knowledge that must be captured and stored. This need, combined with the need to protect intellectual property, makes a powerful case for an increased emphasis on knowledge management.

The Human Side of the Equation

This book's definition of WLP includes the phrase "balancing human, ethical, technological, and operational considerations." This phrase is easy to utter but difficult to put into practice. As WLP departments become better aligned with other business units, their supporters may be tempted to prove the value of WLP to the organization only in terms of cost savings. Although this strategy will help the WLP professional to win recognition as a strategic business partner, it could produce grave effects for the longtime viability of the organization. WLP professionals must walk a precarious line between productivity and humanistic concerns. The phrase "workplace learning and performance is . . ." holds the key to doing this. Notice that what was once two separate concepts has merged into a single entity. Rather than viewing learning and performance improvement in juxtaposition, everyone in an organization must understand that one cannot exist without the other. If an organization overemphasizes performance, it will only reap short-term benefits. If an organization sinks countless dollars into employee education without considering how this education is helping to make the employees more competitive in the future, then profitability will surely drop. If an organization assumes that a lack of employee knowledge causes all performance problems, then systemic issues such as a broken process will continue to plague the organization, and highly skilled workers will defect to competing organizations.

As the line managers pointed out in their qualitative responses, the key challenge that organizations will continue to face in the future is recruiting, educating, motivating, and retaining good employees—especially during times of low unemployment. This desire to create and maintain a high-performance workforce drives WLP.

At the crux of this matter, however, is the crucial need to motivate employees. WLP professionals must begin to acknowledge that they cannot instill motivation in a person, but rather people must motivate themselves. All that an external person can do is try to create an environment conducive to higher levels of motivation. This task is not easy because learners' motivations vary tremendously. As Alfie Kohn (1995) points out in his book *Punished by Rewards*, many factors affect human behavior, and these factors are constantly changing. Unlike the Skinnerian view of behavior, Kohn's view is that people—unlike rats and pigeons in Skinner's example—will always respond the same way to an identical stimulus. Even a well-designed incentive program will not forever motivate people to produce the desired result. The reality is that people's expectations change constantly, and therefore the environment that will motivate them must change constantly as well. Anil D. Savkar, a line manager respondent from Booz, Allen & Hamilton, Inc., stated that "receiving a reward may have short-term, positive, and motivational impact, but the absence of reward can have long-term, de-motivational impact. Motivation will be a key ingredient, and its study will be a future trend." Many line managers and executives find this concept difficult to grasp. They may be accustomed to implementing a policy and expecting it to produce the same results year after year.

This lack of understanding will compound the problem of balancing organizational and humanistic concerns further. An astute WLP professional will constantly monitor the pulse of the organization and help the organization's leader deal with change proactively. In their qualitative responses, many line managers mentioned the importance of helping "the organization adapt to change." This point will not surprise anyone who has worked in a front-line business unit.

The Global Future

People from 28 countries participated in this study. Although the Web made this economical and efficient, the motivation behind using the technology is important. Why would people from all over the world be interested in WLP? Elaborate data are not necessary to answer this question. Work is one of the few common denominators between all people of the world. As Karl Marx pointed out in the *Communist Manifesto*, work is one of the central activities in life that give people a sense of identity. If the work experience is degrading and meaningless, a person's sense of personal worth may suffer. If the workplace provides an environment in which accomplishment and learning can flourish, however, the employee's sense of self-worth will be fostered. WLP will continue to be a central part of the human experience, because it represents a large part of an employee's life. As the marketplace and society become more globally oriented, the need for balancing humanistic and ethical considerations will increase exponentially. Working to find common ground with people on the other side of the world will challenge and expand everyone's social norms.

Adaptive-oriented learning: Future-oriented learning that occurs through reflection, discovery, and innovative thinking and usually involves the generation of new ideas and new approaches.

Action planning: A change process stage in which a change agent works with a group to clarify what action they should take to solve the problem or seize the opportunity confronting the group.

Action research: A model of what occurs in a change process; the foundation for most organization development interventions.

Assessment and feedback: A change process stage in which a change agent collects information from group members—individually or collectively—regarding their perceptions of problems or improvement opportunities confronting the group.

Career development: A discipline "focused on assuring an alignment of individual career planning and organization career-management processes to achieve an optimal match of individual and organizational needs" (McLagan, 1989, p. 7).

Cause analysis: The process of isolating the cause—or causes—of a gap between the actual and ideal level of performance.

Change champion: A leader with the vision to see that something new is needed.

Change driver: An impetus for change; a reason to learn or to improve performance.

Change management: The process of providing continuing oversight of the change implementation process and helping the organization adapt to changes.

Change sponsor: A leader with the vision, power, and resources needed to make change.

Codes of conduct: See **Codes of ethics.**

Codes of ethics: A description of how individuals who work in an occupation, organization, or field of practice should—or should not—behave.

Competency: "An area of knowledge or skill that is critical for producing key outputs; . . . internal capabilities that people bring to their jobs; capabilities which may be expressed in a broad, even infinite array of on-the-job behaviors" (McLagan, 1989, p. 77).

Corporate restructuring: The de-layering, business re-engineering, and process improvement of organizations.

Development: A long-term change strategy that makes use of individuals as instruments for organizational learning.

Entry: The point at which an external or internal change agent arrives to help facilitate a change effort.

Environmental scanning: The process of continuously monitoring changing conditions in the external environment.

Ethical breach: Failure to live up to one's moral principles.

Ethical issues: "Key areas of ethical challenge that HRD practitioners frequently face" (McLagan, 1989, p. 77).

Ethics: A term derived from the Latin word for character and referring to principles of right and wrong.

Evaluation: Examination of results and assessment of the extent of their impact.

Goal clarity: Agreement by decision makers and stakeholders on the results sought from a change effort.

Goal displacement: A loss of focus on the intended results.

High-performance workplace (HPW): An organization that provides a climate in which individuals and groups can function to peak performance.

Human performance improvement (HPI): "The systematic process of discovering and analyzing important human performance gaps, planning for future improvements in human performance, designing and developing cost-effective and ethically-justifiable interventions to close performance gaps, implementing the interventions, and evaluating the financial and nonfinancial results" (Rothwell, 1996a, p. 79).

Human resource development (HRD): "The integrated use of Training and Development, Organization Development, and Career Development to improve individual, group, and organizational effectiveness" (McLagan, 1989, p. 7).

Instructional systems design (ISD): A systematic approach to planning instruction. ISD has been described in over 40 models. Most of the models share common characteristic steps: analyze needs, design instruction, develop and deliver instruction, and evaluate results.

Instructional technology: The applications of technology to instruction.

Intellectual capital: An organization's knowledge that is composed of human capital, structural capital, and customer capital.

Intervention implementation: The process of applying the intervention. (In a learning intervention, the process of delivering the instruction to the learner or providing the learner with his or her own means to learn. In a management intervention, the process of putting the planned change into effect.)

Intervention selection: A strategy for improving performance or solving a performance problem.

ISD: See **Instructional systems design.**

Knowledge management: The process and methods of collecting, organizing, and disseminating intellectual capital.

Learning: The process of acquiring new knowledge and skills, changing behavior or attitudes based on developing new ways of thinking, and inventing new approaches.

Learning organization: An organization that supports and fosters learning.

Learning-oriented interventions: Interventions focused on changing people by equipping them with new knowledge, skills, or attitudes.

Maintenance-oriented learning: Past- and present-oriented learning that is based on experience and usually involves mastery of what is already known.

Management interventions: Interventions focused on changing the work environment that rely on management and employee action as a key approach to bringing about change and improving performance.

Morals: Knowing and applying principles of right and wrong.

Organization development: A discipline "focused on assuring healthy inter- and intra-unit relationships and helping groups initiate and manage change" (McLagan, 1989, p. 7).

Open system: A system characterized by inputs (such as people, capital, or information) and transformed through processes (such as work methods or procedures) into outputs (such as products or services).

Output: "A product or service that an individual or group delivers to others, especially to colleagues, customers, or clients" (McLagan, 1989, p. 77).

Performance: The achievement of effective outcomes from productive work.

Performance analysis: The process of detecting gaps between actual and ideal performance.

Performance management: A continuing effort, conducted proactively, to inform people of performance goals, recommend ways to achieve those goals, supply incentives and rewards for performance, and supply ways to define and measure success.

Productivity paradox: The dilemma in which the hoped-for gains expected from technology end up disappointingly lower than anticipated.

Research agenda: A long-range plan to guide research.

Role: "A common grouping of competencies. A role should not be confused with a job title" (McLagan, 1989, p. 77).

Sociotechnical systems: The integration of technology and human social structures.

Start-up: The point in a change process at which the change agent works with the group to become familiar with the background of the organization, group, or people who are targeted for the change effort.

Subsystem: Part of a system.

Suprasystem: The external environment surrounding an open system.

Technology: Tools, equipment, and work methods; the know-how to use them.

Training: A short-term change strategy geared to equipping individuals with new knowledge and skills.

Trend: A force for change; a pattern of events noticeable over time.

Values: The core set of beliefs of an individual or a group.

Workplace learning and performance (WLP): The integrated use of learning and other interventions for the purpose of improving individual and organizational performance. It uses a systematic process of analyzing performance and responding to individual, group, and organizational needs. WLP creates positive, progressive change within organizations by balancing human, ethical, technological, and operational considerations.

BIBLIOGRAPHY

Adams, A. (1997). Educational attainment. *Current Population Reports,* Series P20–476, U.S. Bureau of the Census. [From the Web Site of the U.S. Bureau of the Census.]

Appelbaum, E. and Batt, R. (1994). *The new American workplace: Transforming work systems in the United States.* Ithaca, NY: ILR Press.

Atwater, D. and Niehaus, R. (1993). Diversity implications for an occupation human resource forecast for the year 2000. *Human Resource Planning, 16(4),* 29–50.

Barley, S. (1994). Technology and the future of work. *Administrative Science Quarterly, 39(1),* 183–186.

Barnum, P. (1991). Misconceptions about the future U.S. work force: Implications for strategic planning. *Human Resource Planning, 14(3),* 209–219.

Bassi, L.; Buchanan, L.; and Cheney, S. (1997a). *Trends that affect learning and performance improvement: A report on the members of the ASTD benchmarking forum.* Alexandria, VA: The American Society for Training & Development.

Bassi, L.; Cheney S.; and Van Buren, M. (1997b). Training industry trends 1997. *Training & Development,* November, 46–59.

Bassi, L.; Gould, E.; Kulik, J.; and Zornitsky, J. (1993). *Thinking outside the lines: High performance companies in manufacturing and services.* Cambridge, MA: ABT.

Becker, S. (1977). Analyzing organizational performance. *Training, 14(6),* 49–50.

Bengtson, B. *An analysis of CEO perceptions concerning trainer roles in selected central Pennsylvania manufacturing firms.* Unpublished doctoral dissertation. University Park: The Pennsylvania State University, 1994.

Bennett, A. (1988). Ethics codes spread despite criticism. *The Wall Street Journal* (15 June).

Benveniste, G. (1994). *The twenty-first century organization: Analyzing current trends, imagining the future.* San Francisco: Jossey-Bass.

Berenbeim, R. (1991). *Corporate ethics: A research report from The Conference Board.* New York: The Conference Board.

Bolt, J. and Rummler, G. (1982). How to close the gap in human performance. *Management Review, 71(1),* 38–44.

Brethower, D. (1995). Specifying the human performance technology knowledgebase. *Performance Improvement Quarterly, 8(2),* 17–39.

Brewster, C. and Hegewisch, A. (1993). A contingent of diversity. *Personnel Management, 25(1),* 36–40.

Brock, M. (1996). Future forces. In W. Rothwell, *The ASTD models for human performance improvement.* Alexandria, VA: ASTD.

Brookfield, S. (1996). *Understanding and facilitating adult learning.* San Francisco: Jossey-Bass.

Brooking, A. (1996). *Intellectual capital.* London: International Thomson Business.

Brown, M. (1986). Analyzing consequences for improving organizational performance—Part 1. *Performance and Instruction Journal, 25(10),* 26–29.

Brown, M. (1987). Analyzing consequences for improving organizational performance—Part 2. *Performance and Instruction, 26(2),* 31–33.

Brown, M. (1990). You get what you measure: Engineering a performance measurement system. *Performance and Instruction, 29(5),* 11–16.

Brown, M. and Schwarz, J. (1988). What to fix when everything's broken. *Performance and Instruction, 27(4),* 6–11.

Business students cheat most. (1991). *Fortune* (1 July).

Businesses are signing up for ethics 101. (1988). *Business Week* (15 February).

Cameron, W. (1988). *Training competencies of human resource development specialists in Tennessee.* (Summary Report, Research Series No. 1). Knoxville: University of Tennessee.

Campbell, P. (1996). *Population projections for states by age, sex, race, and Hispanic origin: 1995 to 2025.* PPL-47.

Carnevale, A. and Carnevale, E. (1994a). Growth patterns in workplace training. *Training & Development,* 48(5), S22–28.

Carnevale, A. and Carnevale, E. (1994b). Trends in training on the job. *Technical & Skills Training,* 5(4), 10–16.

Carnevale, A.; Gainer, L.; and Villet, J. (1990). *Training in America: The organization and strategic role of training.* San Francisco: Jossey-Bass.

Cascio, W. (1993). Downsizing: What do we know? What have we learned? *Academy of Management Executive,* 7(1).

Catten, P. (1993). The diversity of Hispanics in the U.S. work force. *Monthly Labor Review,* 116(8), 3–15.

Cavanagh, G.; Moberg, D.; and Velasquez, M. (1981). The ethics of organizational politics. *Academy of Management Review,* 6, 363–374.

Chevalier, R. (1990). Analyzing performance discrepancies with line managers. *Performance and Instruction,* 29(10), 23–26.

Church, A. From both sides now organizational downsizing. What is the role of the practitioner? Available from http://www.css.edu/users/dswenson/web/dnsizes/htm.

Competency Standards Body—Assessors & Workplace Trainers. (1994). *Workplace trainer competency standards.* Australia: Competency Standards Body—Assessors & Workplace Trainers.

Cross, K. (1981). *Adults as learners: Increasing participation and facilitating learning.* San Francisco: Jossey-Bass.

Dean, Peter J. (1996). Ethics and human performance improvement. In William J. Rothwell, *ASTD Models for Human Performance Improvement.* Alexandria, VA: ASTD.

Deaner, C. and Dick, M. (1994). A model of organization development ethics. *Public Administration Quarterly,* 17(4), 435–446.

Dixon, V.; Conway, K.; Ashley, K.; and Stewart, N. (1995). *Training competency architecture* and *Training competency architecture toolkit.* Toronto: Ontario Society for Training and Development.

Dubois, D. and Rothwell, W. (1996a). *Developing the high performance workplace administrator's handbook.* Amherst, MA: Human Resource Development Press.

Dubois, D. and Rothwell, W. (1996b). *Developing the high performance workplace organizational assessment instrument.* Amherst, MA: Human Resource Development Press.

Edvinsson, L. and Malone, M. (1997). *Intellectual capital: Realizing your company's true value.* New York: HarperCollins.

Eubanks, J.; Marshall, J.; and Driscoll, M. (1990). A competency model for OD practitioners. *Training & Development,* 44(11), 85–90.

Foshay, W.; Silber, K.; and Westgaard, O. (1986). *Instructional design competencies: The standards.* Iowa City, IA: The International Board of Standards for Training, Performance and Instruction.

Foshay, W.; Silber, K.; and Westgaard, O. (1990). *Training manager competencies: The standards.* Iowa City, IA: The International Board of Standards for Training, Performance and Instruction.

Frank, E. (1988). An attempt at a definition of HRD. *Journal of European Industrial Training,* 12(5), 4–5.

Fritzche, D. and Becker, H. (1984). Linking management behavior to ethical philosophy—An empirical investigation. *Academy of Management Journal,* 27, 165–175.

Fullerton, H., Jr. (1991). Labor force projections: The baby boom moves on. *Monthly Labor Review,* 114(11), 31–44.

Fullerton, H., Jr. (1993). Another look at the labor force. *Monthly Labor Review,* 116(11), 31–40.

Gayeski, D. (1995). Changing roles and professional challenges for human performance technology. *Performance Improvement Quarterly,* 8(2), 6–16.

Gellerman, S. (1986, July-August). Why "good" managers make bad ethical choices. *Harvard Business Review,* 64, 85–90.

Gilbert, T. (1988). Measuring the potential for performance improvement. *Training,* 25(7), 49–52.

Gilbert, T. and Gilbert, M. (1989). Performance engineering: Making human productivity a science. *Performance and Instruction, 28*(1), 3–9.

Ginkel, K.; Mulder, M.; and Nijhof, W. (1994). Role profiles of HRD professionals in the Netherlands. Paper presented at the conference "Education and Training for Work." Twente: University of Twente.

Ginzberg, E. (1958). *Human resources: The wealth of a nation.* New York: Simon & Schuster.

Harbour, J. (1992). Improving performance: Why we fail sometimes. *Performance and Instruction, 31*(5), 4–9.

Harmon, P. (1984). A hierarchy of performance variables. *Performance and Instruction, 23*(10), 27–28.

Herem, M. (1979). Identifying causes of job performance deficiencies. *Improving Human Performance Quarterly, 8*(1), 53–61.

Hilgert, R. (1989, April). What ever happened to ethics in business and business schools? *The Diary of Alpha Kappa Psi,* 4–7.

Hofstede, G. (1991). *Cultures and organization: Software of the mind.* New York: McGraw-Hill.

Huselid, M. (1993). The impact of environmental volatility on human resource planning and strategic human resource management. *Human Resource Planning, 16*(3), 35–51.

Hutchison, C.; Stein, F.; and Shepherd, J. (1988). *Instructor competencies volume 1: The standards.* Batavia, NY: The International Board of Standards for Training, Performance, and Instruction.

Kirkpatrick, Donald L. (1996). *Evaluating Training Programs: The Four Levels.* San Francisco: Berrett-Koehler.

Kirrane, D. (1990, November). Managing values: A systematic approach to business ethics. *Training & Development Journal, 35*(11), 53–60.

Kohn, Alfie. (1995). *Punished by rewards: The trouble with gold stars, incentive plans, A's, praise, and other bribes.* Boston: Houghton Mifflin Company.

Kouzes, J. and Posner, B. (1987). *The leadership challenge: How to get extraordinary things done in organizations.* San Francisco: Jossey-Bass.

Langlois, C. and Schlegelmilch, B. (1990, Fourth Quarter). Do corporate codes of ethics reflect national character? Evidence from Europe and the United States. *Journal of International Business Studies,* 519–533.

Lawrie, J. (1990). Differentiate between training, education and development. *Personnel Journal, 69*(10), 44.

Leach, J. (1991). Characteristics of excellent trainers: A psychological and interpersonal profile. *Performance Improvement Quarterly, 4*(3), 42–62.

Lee, C. (1985). Human resource development: A useful bit of jargon? *Training, 22*(1), 75–76.

Lee, S. (1994). *A preliminary study of the competencies, work outputs, and roles of human resource development professionals in the Republic of China on Taiwan: A cross-cultural competency study.* Unpublished doctoral dissertation. University Park: The Pennsylvania State University.

Lippitt, G. and Nadler, L. (1967). Emerging roles of the training director. *Training & Development Journal, 21*(8), 26–31.

Longnecker, J.; McKinney, J.; and Moore, C. (1988, Winter). Egoism and independence: Entrepreneurial ethics. *Organizational Dynamics,* 64–72.

Marquardt, M. and Engel, D. (1993a). *Global human resource development.* Englewood Cliffs, NJ: Prentice-Hall.

Marquardt, M. and Engel, D. (1993b). HRD competencies for a shrinking world. *Training & Development, 47*(5), 59–65.

Marx, K. with Friedrich Engels, contributor. (1992). *The Communist Manifesto.* New York: Bantam Books. Originally published in 1848.

MC Associates. (1996). *Managing mergers and acquisitions, best practices report.* Author.

McLagan, P. (1989). *Models for HRD practice.* (4 volumes). Alexandria, VA: ASTD.

McLagan, P. and McCullough, R. (1983). *Models for excellence: The conclusions and recommendations of the ASTD training and development competency study.* Washington, DC: ASTD.

Merriam, S. (1993). An update on adult learning theory. In *New directions for adult and continuing education*. San Francisco: Jossey-Bass.

Merriam-Webster, Incorporated. (1996). *Merriam-Webster's Collegiate Dictionary, Tenth Edition*. Springfield, MA: Author.

Miller, V. (1996). The history of training. In R. Craig (Ed.), *The ASTD training and development handbook: A guide to human resource development*. New York: McGraw-Hill.

Mosier, N. (1988). Human and organizational performance: A model. *Performance and Instruction Journal, 27*(1), 39–43.

Nadler, L. (1962). A study of the needs of selected training directors in Pennsylvania which might be met by professional education institutions. *Dissertation Abstracts International, 24*(2).

Nadler, L. (1980). Defining the field—is it HRD or OD, or ? *Training & Development Journal, 34*(12), 66–68.

Naisbitt, J. (1994). *Global paradox*. New York: Avon Books.

National Association of Manufacturers. (1991). *Today's dilemma: Tomorrow's competitive edge: Learning from the NAM/Towers Perrin skills gap survey*. Washington, DC: Author.

Nonaka, R. and Takeuchi, H. (1995). *The knowledge-creating company: How Japanese companies create the dynamics of innovation*. New York: Oxford University Press.

Office of the American Workplace. (1995). *The road to high performance workplaces*. Washington, DC: U.S. Department of Labor.

Ontario Society for Training and Development. (1976). *Core competencies for training and development*. Toronto: Ontario Society for Training and Development.

Ornstein, S. and Isabella, L. (1993). Making sense of careers: A review 1989–1992. *Journal of Management, 19*(2), 243–267.

Owens, J. (1989). *Ethical theory and business decisions* (2nd edition). Arlington, VA: Management Education, Ltd.

Pace University study. (1998). *Academy of Management Executive 12*(1) 58–63.

Perry, D.; Bennett, K.; and Edwards, G. (1990). *Ethics policies and programs in American business*. Washington, DC: Ethics Resource Center.

Petrick, J. and Pullins, E. (1992). Organizational ethics development and the expanding role of the human resource professional. *Health Care Supervisor, 11*(2), 59.

Pinto, P. and Walker, J. (1978). *A study of professional training and development roles and competencies*. Madison, WI: The American Society for Training & Development.

Piskurich, G. and Sanders, E. (1998). *ASTD models for learning technologies: Roles, competencies, and outputs*. Alexandria, VA: ASTD.

Rae, L. (1993). *Evaluating trainer effectiveness*. New York: Business-One.

Rice, D. and Drelinger, C. (1990, May). Rights and wrongs of ethics training. *Training & Development Journal, 35*(5), 103–109.

Rijk, R.; Mulder, M.; and Nijhof, W. (1994). *Role profiles of HRD practitioners in 4 European countries*. A paper presented in Milan, Italy. Twente: University of Twente.

Roddick, A. (1991). Make morality the goal. *Fortune* (30 December).

Rosow, J. and Hickey, J. (1994). *Strategic partners for high performance: Part I: The partnership paradigm for competitive advantage*. Scarsdale, NY: The Work in America Institute.

Rothwell, W. (1996a). *The ASTD models for human performance improvement*. Alexandria, VA: ASTD.

Rothwell, W. (1996b). *Beyond training and development: State-of-the-art strategies for enhancing human performance*. New York: AMACOM.

Rothwell, W. and Cookson, P. (1997). *Beyond instruction: Comprehensive program planning for business and education*. San Francisco: Jossey-Bass.

Rothwell, W. and Kazanas, H. (1998). *Mastering the instructional design process: A systematic approach* (2nd edition). San Francisco: Jossey-Bass.

Rothwell, W. and Sredl, H. (1992). *The ASTD reference guide to professional human resource development roles and competencies* (2nd edition, 2 volumes). Amherst, MA: Human Resource Development Press.

Rothwell, W.; Sullivan, R.; and McLean, G. (1995a). *Practicing organization development: A guide for consultants*. San Diego: Pfeiffer & Co.

Rothwell, W.; Sullivan, R.; and McLean, G. (1995b). Models for change and steps in action research. In W. Rothwell, R. Sullivan and G. McLean (Eds.), *Practicing organization development: A guide for consultants*. San Diego: Pfeiffer & Co.

Rummler, G. (1990). *Improving performance: How to manage the white space on the organization chart*. San Francisco: Jossey-Bass.

Schechter, S.; Rothwell, W.; and McLane, S. (1996, June 19). Think tank uses reverse delphi process to reach consensus on top trends/competencies. *Issues & Trends in Personnel*, Issue No. 382, 8–9.

Schmidt, W. and Posner, B. (1982). *Managerial values and expectations: The silent power in personal and organizational life*. New York: AMACOM.

Senge, P. (1990). *The Fifth Discipline: The Art and Practice of the Learning Organization*. New York: Bantam Doubleday Dell Publishing Group, Inc.

Shea, G. (1988). *Practical ethics*. New York: AMACOM.

Silvestri, G. (1993). Occupational employment: Wide variations in growth. *Monthly Labor Review, 116*(11), 58–86.

Stewart, T. (1997). *Intellectual capital: The new wealth of organizations*. New York: Doubleday.

Stolovich, H. and Keeps, E. (Eds.) (1992). *Handbook of human performance technology: A comprehensive guide for analyzing and solving performance problems in organizations*. San Francisco: Jossey-Bass.

Stolovich, H.; Keeps, E.; and Rodrigue, D. (1995). Skills sets for the human performance technologist. *Performance Improvement Quarterly, 8*(2), 40–67.

Strange, T. (1993). The future of work: The human organization. *Management-Auckland, 40*(10), 45–49.

Subermanian, R. (1993). Environmental scanning in U.S. companies: Their nature and their relationship to performance. *Management International Review, 33*(3), 271–286.

Sveiby, K. (1997). *The new organizational wealth: Managing and measuring knowledge-based assets*. San Francisco: Berrett-Koehler.

Sweeney, R. (1990). Survey: Ethics in corporate America. *Management Accounting* (June).

Training & Development Lead Body. (1992). *National Standards for Training and Development*. England: Training & Development Lead Body.

Trevino, L. (1990). A cultural perspective on changing and developing organizational ethics. In R. Woodman and W. Pasmore (Eds.), *Research in organizational change and development*. Greenwich, CT: JAI Press.

Ulrich, D.; Brockbank, W.; and Yeung, A. (1989). HR competencies in the 1990s. *Personnel Administrator, 34*(11), 91–93.

U.S. Civil Service Commission. (1976). *The employee development specialist curriculum plan: An outline of learning experiences for the employee development specialist*. Washington, DC: Author.

U.S. Department of Labor. (1992). *Bulletin 2401: Occupational projections and training data*. Washington, DC: Author.

U.S. Department of Labor. (1993). *The secretary's commission on achieving necessary skills and tasks for jobs: A SCANS report for America 2000*. Washington, DC: Author.

USA Today (1998, 4 June).

Walton, C. (1990). *The moral manager*. New York: Harper Business.

Watkins, K. (1991). Many voices: Defining human resource development from different disciplines. *Adult Education Quarterly, 41*(4), 241–255.

Watkins, K. and Marsick, V. (1993). *Sculpting the learning organization: Lessons in the art and science of systemic change.* San Francisco: Jossey-Bass.

Weber, J. (1991). Adapting Kohlberg to enhance the assessment of manager's moral reasoning. *Business Ethics Quarterly, 1*(3), 293–319.

Welton, R. (1993). Understanding ethics development and employee behavior. *Internal Auditing, 8*(3), 63–69.

Wiatrowski, W. (1994). Small businesses and their employees. *Monthly Labor Review, 117*(10), 29–35.

Yelin, E. and Katz, P. (1994). Labor force trends of persons with and without disabilities. *Monthly Labor Review, 117*(10), 36–42.

The responses that the line manager or expert groups repeated at least two times are listed below. The questions are also provided for reference.

Line Manager Responses

Trends

Please identify what you consider to be the significant future trends in the American workplace which will most profoundly affect the role and/or job success of workplace learning and performance professionals over the next five years.

- Increased diversity in the workforce
- Increased amount of telecommuting
- Increased need to stay current with technology
- Increased amount of outsourcing
- Increased reliance on technology and automation in the workplace
- Increased need for internal training programs
- Increased amount of turnover
- Increased need for self-directed work teams
- Increased global competition
- Increased difficulty in attracting good employees in the face of low unemployment
- Decreased competency in the general workforce

WLP's Future Role

What do you foresee as the primary role(s) of workplace learning and performance over the next five years?

- Creating a positive culture to boost employee retention and recruitment
- Finding ways to help train and manage telecommuters
- Preparing the organization for change
- Delivering more learning via electronic means
- Educating senior management about best practices in human resources
- Designing and implementing rewards and recognition programs that promote higher performance
- Helping employees become accountable for their own learning
- Improving human performance using holistic and systematic approaches that solve problems

Expert Responses

Trends

Please identify what you consider to be the significant future trends in the American workplace which will most pro- *foundly affect the role and/or job success of workplace learning and performance professionals over the next five years.*

- Mergers and acquisitions—impact on culture, organizational learning
- Outsourcing
- Knowledge management, data overload
- Measurement of knowledge capital
- Production of high-quality, customized processes, short time
- Increased dependence on technological trends
- Globalization of workplace issues (social agenda in business)
- Industry/educational challenges, impacting leadership, management styles
- Increased number of democracies in progress (globalization)
- Proactive responsiveness to customer needs
- Technology impact on delivery of goods and services
- Downsizing organizational development and training staffs
- Complexity of organizations and inter-organizational configurations
- Integration of competencies into rewards and compensation

WLP's Future Role

What do you foresee as the primary role(s) of workplace learning and performance over the next five years?

- Creating a framework for applying knowledge management
- Lead cultural change/diversity
- Confronting complex business changes, strategic planning
- Creating national methodology for organizations to survive
- Going beyond perceived limits to understand/affect performance and enhance workplace learning
- Designing systems to capitalize on human potential
- Acquiring skill, knowledge, and learning
- Building organizations that meet changing business demands
- Acting as keeper/disseminator of intellectual property and capital management
- Leading the transition from learning—performance—business results, outcomes
- Creating competitive advantages in knowledge and service businesses
- Making the transition to global leadership position
- Building networks and strategic alternatives that foster effective use of resources

1770: The Industrial Revolution begins.

1772: Josiah Wedgwood, an English potter and the inventor of Wedgwood ware, experiments with industrial quality control.

1800s: The Industrial Revolution moves work from the individual, family, or small group to the emerging corporate organization. Training people to work at specific tasks becomes a necessity.

1809: The Masonic Grand Lodge of New York, under De Witt Clinton, establishes vocational training facilities.

1830: Columbia University establishes a new curriculum for young men "employed in business and mercantile establishments."

1862: The Morill Act, signed by U.S. president Abraham Lincoln, establishes land-grant agricultural and mechanical colleges. County extension agents begin to train farmers to improve productivity.

1872: Hoe and Company of New York opens one of the first factory schools.

1880: Christopher Langdell introduces the case method at Harvard Law School.

1883: A German adult educator coins the term "andragogy," referring to adult learning.

1906: The National Society for the Promotion of Industrial Education is formed.

1910: J. L. Moreno introduces role play and psychodrama in Vienna, Austria.

1911: Frederick W. Taylor publishes *The Principles of Scientific Management*.

1916: Henri Fayol declares that the work of managers is to plan, organize, coordinate, and control.

1917: Charles R. Allen uses the "show, tell, do, check" method to train 50,000 shipyard workers.

1920s: Unions set up their first training programs for employees. Bell Labs introduces total quality management (TQM) and statistical quality control.

1924: Joseph M. Juran begins his work on managing quality.

1925: Mary Parker Follett develops the law of the situation, emphasizing human factors in management and recommending joint business planning between leaders and subordinates.

1926: *The Meaning of Adult Education*, by Eduard C. Lindeman, challenges the notion that the pedagogical model of education is appropriate for adults.

1927: The Hawthorne Experiments, at the Western Electric Plant in Cicero, Illinois, reveal the influences of physical and psychological factors on productivity.

1931: Professor Erwin H. Schell initiates the M.I.T. Executive Development program—the first "away-from-company" program for executives.

1933: The Wagner-Peyser Act creates the U.S. Employment Service.

1936: Dale Carnegie publishes *How to Win Friends and Influence People*.

1938: U.S. president Franklin D. Roosevelt signs an executive order stating that the government, as an employer, should provide training for its employees.

1940: The first train-the-trainer programs for supervisors are developed by the Training Within Industry Service of the War Manpower Commission. Known as J programs, they cover job instruction training, job relations training, job methods training, and job safety training.

1942: Peter Drucker publishes his first book, *The Future of Industrial Man: A Conservative Approach*.

1942: The American Society for Training Directors (ASTD) is formed on April 2, 1942, at a meeting of the American Petroleum Institute, in New Orleans, Louisiana. Fifteen training directors hold their first meeting on January 12, 1943, in Baton Rouge.

1943: Abraham Maslow publishes *A Theory of Human Motivation*.

1944: The G. I. Bill of Rights is signed making grants and loans for college available to U.S. military personnel.

1945: ASTD publishes the first issue of *Industrial Training News*, a quarterly publication that is eventually to become *Training & Development* magazine.

1946: Kurt Lewin first experiments with group dynamics at the Connecticut Interracial Commission.

1947: National Training Laboratories conducts its first session in human relations training, also known as sensitivity training or T-group training.

1947: *Industrial Training News* changes its name to *Journal of Industrial Training* and becomes a bimonthly periodical.

1950: American quality experts Joseph M. Juran and W. Edwards Deming go to Japan as advisors on the reconstruction of Japanese industry.

1951: *Total Quality Control*, by A. V. Feigenbaum, is published.

1951: ASTD opens its first permanent office in Madison, Wisconsin, the hometown of Russell Moberly, the secretary-treasurer who keeps all the records at the time.

1952: ASTD membership reaches 1,600. There are 32 ASTD chapters across the country.

1953: B. F. Skinner's *Science and Human Behavior* is published, introducing the idea of behavior modification.

1954: *Journal of Industrial Training* changes name to *The Journal of the American Society of Training Directors*.

1956: IBM opens the first residential executive-development facility at Sands Point on Long Island, New York.

1958: Responding to the USSR's launch of Sputnik, the U.S. government signs the National Defense Education Act.

1959: ASTD's *Journal of Industrial Training* changes its name to *Training Directors Journal* and publishes Donald L. Kirkpatrick's article establishing four levels of evaluation for training: reaction, learning, behavior, and results.

1959: The U.S. Chamber of Commerce introduces the Action Course in Practical Politics. Corporate trainers are responsible for this popular effort to encourage employees to be active in political parties.

1960: Douglas M. McGregor's *The Human Side of Enterprise* is published, describing Theory X and Theory Y as opposing viewpoints of people's fundamental perceptions of work.

1961: *Sloan Management Review* publishes Edgar H. Schein's "Management Development as a Process of Influences."

1961: ASTD begins publication of *Training Research Abstracts*, later incorporated into *Training & Development Journal*.

1962: Congress votes into law the Manpower Development and Training Act (MDTA).

1962: The National Society for Performance and Instruction is formed.

1962: The National Testing Service publishes the Myers-Briggs psychological type indicator.

1964: ASTD changes its name to the American Society for Training and Development.

1966: *Training Directors Journal* changes its name to *Training and Development Journal*.

1967: McGraw-Hill publishes the first edition of *ASTD's Training and Development Handbook*.

1968: ASTD membership reaches 7,422. There are 65 chapters.

1968: The term *Human Resource Development* is coined by Leonard Nadler during a class he is teaching at The George Washington University in Washington, D.C.

1970: The NTL Institute for Behavioral Science announces it will build "the world's first university devoted entirely to applied behavioral science."

1970: The new U.S. Occupational Safety and Heath Administration mandates safety education and training for workers.

1971: *Management Science* publishes Henry Mintzberg's "Managerial Work: Analysis From Observation," describing managerial work in terms of 10 roles and challenging Henri Fayol's 1916 definition.

1972: ASTD and the U.S. State Department (AID) sponsor the first international training and development conference in Geneva, Switzerland. Two hundred people from six continents attend.

1973: The International Federation of Training and Development Organizations is formed, with ASTD's assistance, through a grant from the Agency for International Development.

1973: Comprehensive Employment and Training Act (CETA) enacted. CETA provides public service employment and subsidized on-the-job training for the disadvantaged.

1973: Malcolm Knowles's *The Adult Learner: A Neglected Species* is published.

1974: *Changing Supervisor Behavior,* by A. P. Goldstein and M. Sorcher, is published, linking behavioral modeling to training.

1975: ASTD opens a branch office in Washington, D.C.

1978: ASTD membership reaches 15,323; chapters number 110.

1978: Section 127 of the Revenue Act of 1978 is enacted. The law excluded from taxable income employer-sponsored educational assistance for any type of course.

1978: Following ASTD's efforts in Congress, the Employee Education Assistance IRS exemption is approved.

1978: International Society for Performance Improvement publishes Thomas Gilbert's book titled *Human Competence.*

1978: ASTD publishes its first study of competencies titled *Study of Professional Training and Development Roles and Competencies*, by Pinto and Walker.

1981: ASTD moves its headquarters from Madison, Wisconsin, to Washington, D.C.

1981: Kenneth Blanchard and Spencer Johnson publish *The One Minute Manager.*

1982: Tom Peters and Robert Waterman publish *In Search of Excellence.*

1983: The National Commission on Excellence in Education publishes *A Nation at Risk.*

1983: Job Training Partnership Act enacted. Congress passes this act to provide training and employment assistance to disadvantaged and dislocated workers.

1983: McLagan's and McCullough's competency study *Models for Excellence* is published by ASTD.

1983: ASTD publishes monographs *Human Capital* and *Investment and Employee Training* outlining economic data to prove economic growth and prosperity depend on investing in training.

1984: ASTD implements a new governance structure, resulting in a new leadership direction for the Board of Directors and the creation of a Board of Governors to look at the future.

1985: ASTD publishes *Jobs for the Nation* describing the impact of training on the U.S. economy.

1986: ASTD succeeds in getting U.S. Congress to approve National Job Skills Week.

1987: George S. Odiorne publishes *The Human Side of Management.*

1987: ASTD launches a new national conference on technical and skills training.

1987: The Malcolm Baldrige National Quality Award is established.

1987: ASTD establishes a research function and receives a $750,000 grant from the U.S. Department of Labor; research grants to ASTD will reach almost $3 million by 1993.

1987: The Hudson Institute publishes *Workforces 2000: Work and Workers for the 21st Century*, by William B. Johnston and Arnold H. Packer. Based on research funded by the U.S. Department of Labor, the report spurs business and government leaders to reevaluate workforce-related policies.

1988: ASTD membership reaches 24,500. There are 150 chapters.

1989: ASTD publishes *Models for HRD Practice* by Patricia McLagan, its first competency study which defines the field of human resource development.

1990: ASTD and the U.S. Department of Labor publish *The Learning Enterprise*, by Anthony P. Carnevale and Leila J. Gainer, as well as the more comprehensive *Training in America: The Organization and Strategic Role of Training*, by Carnevale, Gainer, and Janice Villet. Both works establish the size and score of the training enterprise in the United States.

1990: ASTD launches a new magazine, *Technical & Skills Training*.

1990: Peter M. Senge publishes *The Fifth Discipline: The Art and Practice of the Learning Organization*.

1990: *HRD Quarterly* research journal is jointly published by ASTD, Jossey-Bass, and University of Minnesota.

1991: ASTD publishes *America and the New Economy*, by ASTD's chief economist, Anthony Patrick Carnevale, establishing the economic link between learning and performance.

1991: *Training and Development Journal* becomes *Training & Development*. Circulation tops 34,000 worldwide.

1992: ASTD establishes Benchmarking Forum.

1992: ASTD's Public Policy Council is created.

1993: U.S. president Bill Clinton creates the Office of Work-Based Learning within the Department of Labor.

1994: ASTD launches ASTD Online, an electronic information access service.

1994: ASTD holds its 50th annual conference, the first that's international, in Anaheim, California.

1994: Congress enacts Goals 2000: Educate America Act and School-to-Work Opportunities Act. Goals 2000 provides federal funds to states and local school districts to improve education. School-to-Work provides federal funds to create systems to help transition youth from school to work.

1996: ASTD publishes *ASTD Models for Human Performance Improvement*, a competency study by William J. Rothwell.

1997: ASTD publishes *Responding to Workplace Change: A National Vision for a System for Continuous Learning* by Mary McCain and Cynthia Pantazis. The report outlines national recommendations to improve federal employment and training programs and establish a system of continuous learning for all Americans.

1998: ASTD launches "The Virtual Community" on its Web site (www.astd.org). This service allows ASTD members the chance to network, show, and locate information via the Web.

1998: ASTD begins offering the six-course series Human Performance in the Workplace.

1998: Congress enacts Workforce Investment Act. ASTD successfully works with Congress on a new federal job training reform law that enables states and local governments to develop customer-driven employment and training systems.

1998: ASTD publishes *ASTD Models for Learning Technologies* by George M. Piskurich and Ethan S. Sanders.

1998: ASTD begins co-sponsorship with the Society for Applied Learning Technologies of the "Interactive Multimedia" conferences.

1998: After 18 years of serving as ASTD president, Curtis E. Plott retires from ASTD, and Laura Liswood replaces him as the new president.

1999: ASTD publishes *ASTD Models for Workplace Learning and Performance* by William J. Rothwell, Ethan S. Sanders, and Jeffrey Soper.